HOMEWORK

Homework

*Required Reading
for Teachers and Parents*

GLORIA CHANNON

OUTERBRIDGE & DIENSTFREY
NEW YORK

DISTRIBUTED BY E.P. DUTTON & COMPANY

Library of Congress number 70–126585
First published in the United States of America
in 1970
Copyright © 1970 Outerbridge & Dienstfrey. All rights reserved including the right of reproduction in whole or in part in any form.

Design: Anne Hallowell

Outerbridge & Dienstfrey
200 West 72 Street New York 10023

CONTENTS

I

	Seth	3
	Reading	3
1.	**The Teacher**	**4**
	Math	10
	Luis	11
	Shelley	11
2.	**Freedom**	**12**
	Pupil Routines and Requirements	22
	Going to the Bathroom	24
3.	**Planning, Teaching, Learning**	**25**
	The Arts and Crafts Crew	31
	The World of Adults	32
4.	**On-the-Job Training**	**33**
	Teachers	40
	Little Boxes	41

5.	**On Discipline, Fighting, and Becoming a Group**	**42**
	Teachers as Students	56
	Julio	57
	Art	58
6.	**Battleground and Stalemate**	**60**
	The Classroom as Ritual	76
	Science	77
	Language	77
	Holdovers	77
	Busywork	78
7.	**Avoidance of Failure**	**79**
	Julio	95
	Supervisory Memorandum	95
	The Model Bulletin Board	96
8.	**One World**	**97**
	The Girls	103
9.	**Taking Stock**	**105**
	The Last Day	111

II

10.	**The Teacher — Again**	**115**

If a new edition of the work is ever required, I should like to introduce a few words insisting on the duty of seeking all reasonable pleasure and avoiding all pain that can be honourably avoided. I should like to see children taught that they should not say they like things which they do not like, merely because certain other people say they like them, and how foolish it is to say they believe this or that when they understand nothing about it. . . .

The Way of All Flesh
Samuel Butler

SETH

        Seth is insatiable for work and he works hard at everything. He is compulsive, his body tensed as if in the throes of tough physical labor, his face screwed into a frown of concentration. He has a whole repertory of intense frowns for every occasion. His smiles arrive rarely, in a slow, deliberate sequence. First the frown is removed, the face is carefully planed and smoothed, the eyebrows rearranged, the lips relaxed. Finally the smile, as intense and engulfing as the frown that preceded it.

READING

        A third grader brought me his primer. "I can read it. You wanna hear me read it?" "Sure." "How do you wan' me to read it, with the book open or closed?"

1

THE TEACHER

Like so many others, I became a teacher almost as an afterthought. A housewife with young children, living a block away from a college, how could I better fill in the idle hours than by taking some courses in education?

After twelve years in the classrooms of New York City, I find the idea of any other kind of work unthinkable. This is partly for practical reasons, but it is also, I tell myself, because of the nature of the job itself. Not many people are fortunate enough to make a living at socially useful, potentially creative, soul-fulfilling tasks.

But is teaching socially useful or creative? The answer obviously depends on what kind of day, week, or year it has been. More and more often the answer seems to be no.

But it is hard to say why. The teacher, like the doctor in the midst of an epidemic, is so busy with the daily doings that she finds it hard to get some distance between herself and her functions, to see what is happening. As a result, she is vulnerable to each day's experiences in a special transient way. The school vacations are too long and too separated from the classroom to make them the healing and integrating seasons they should be. The critics and the innovators are always outside the teacher's world, somehow alien and irrelevant.

The Teacher

In an effort to see what was happening in my classroom, I kept a log one year, instead of the mandatory plan book. Plan books never really show what is happening in a classroom. At best they hint at the events, as the books come to include modifications and changes in response to conditions which are not, themselves, ever made explicit.

Returning to the log later, I came as a stranger. I did not remember the feelings or many of the incidents recorded in it. Even the children, returning to life briefly on its pages, were strangers, except for one or two. Was it really like that? Reading the notes, I began to realize how the process of recording the events and the feelings had forced me to look at my classroom from a dozen angles, now worrying at a fragment, now trying to put together a global view. But did I learn anything from it? Have I changed at all?

This is a bad day, week, year. I feel as though all the experience counts for nothing at all. The ideas and the ideals have all come unstuck. Nothing fits. Nothing seems to work. I look and, despite the message I clearly wrote to myself in the log, find myself, again, trying to squeeze the kids into silence and into knowing fractions and into copying things off the board neatly as evidence that something is happening, has happened in my classroom.

All that has happened is that once again I have been sucked into the whirlpool, helpless victim not only of the system but of myself.

So I return to the log, to the notes written in anger and contempt and concern, to try to discover what I (a teacher) am. Maybe this time I will be able to understand myself and what is happening. Maybe this time I shall see where I should go.

When I first began to examine the teaching experience, I thought I was viewing it through the eyes of the children. At least, I was trying to do this. After all, they are the ones for whom school exists, aren't they? It seems reasonable to view the school through their eyes.

But the only child whose sight I possessed was the child I had been—timid, shy, conforming, a good student for whom school was a fantasy world. School was the place where the wise and powerful, recognizing my secret dreams and my WORTH, would benignly honor and reward me.

When I came to the classroom as teacher, as one of the adults, I discovered that I was not the wise and powerful person that my teachers had seemed to me. My child's view of the school world had betrayed me. I judged with bitterness the adults around me. I once, after a half-dozen years' experience, wrote my judgment out.

> In her relationships with her supervisors, the teacher is distrusting, critical, hypersensitive, suspicious, hostile. She cannot talk easily with them. She either toadies or becomes aggressively defensive. She is destroyed by the slightest criticism. She is insatiable in her quest for reassurance and praise. Sometimes she asserts her superior qualities so stridently that her listeners, equally sensitive and threatened, tune her out. She does not really believe in her own ideas and talents.
>
> She is constantly backing down or preparing her exits. She is always burning her bridges before her or hitting back first. She is afraid to assert her rights, to insist on her dignity and worth as a person, to demand respect. Should she, rarely, be treated with dignity and respect, she is enveloped in tension and can find release only in retreat and denial.
>
> Her school is an island in the community, as insulated and isolated as were the British colonials in India. Within the school the pattern of isolation persists. She is alone in her room, surrounded by hostile natives, out of touch with her peers. Outside the classroom, she joins small cliques. If she is manipulative and domineering, her clique will contain two or three weak copies of her who give her strength and gain their own in the aura and illusion of her pseudostrength.
>
> The teacher loves to gossip. She loves to complain. She is jealous of her accomplishments, afraid to share her techniques or her professional secrets. She jockeys for position. She is sarcastic, easily hurt. Sometimes she will not talk to another member of the staff for months or years. She expects new

members to approach her first and they, in turn, are hurt when she does not make the first gesture.

If she is threatened by outsiders, whether parent, civil rights group, or supervisors, she will form strong talking alliances with others on the staff. The alliances rarely lead to action. She passes the buck. No single indignity is ever important enough to make an issue of. Her shoptalk is of monsters and geniuses. She is of course responsible only for the latter.

She will, infrequently, praise another teacher. But this is a self-serving device. Either she identifies with the praiseworthy one or, with becoming modesty, claims a part in the development of the praised person, or she finds praise a socially acceptable technique for ranking out a third person (the auditor) by indirection.

She has no interest in ideas. She pretends to an interest in methods, but only because she seeks panaceas. She confuses improvements in working conditions with radical educational innovations. She is often but not always prejudiced. She tends to be conservative-Democrat in her politics and in New York City was antiunion until the short strike of 1967 showed how safe it was to be in favor of it.

She has very little patience for the classical masochists on the staff, the victims, the losers, the ones who bear the brunt of administrative criticism and persecution, the ones who are loaded down with the dirty jobs: permanent morning duty or audio-visual aids or books-and-supplies or, until the union contract changed the practice, the roughest classes.

She is quite interested in talk about furniture or clothes or shopping. She diets at noon according to every fad and gorges herself at night, fodder for the next day's lunchtime conversation. She is critical of the men on the staff and associates with them as little as possible. She may work in a school for years and not know by name people whose classes are on a different floor or who do not share her lunchroom. She rarely drinks. When she does, she often will regale her listeners with mildly scandalous anecdotes about her students or their families. She is, usually, quite Victorian in her judgments of her students' and their families' morals, while finding some malicious pleasure in their real or imagined improprieties. She often finds it necessary to take tranquilizers or barbiturates.

But she is not lazy. She works like a dog. She fills out reading cards and duplicate office records, book inventories, lunch lists, class photo lists, state census forms, report cards, reports by the hundred. She used to correct standardized tests, although her supervisors often would not let her correct those of her own class (in which she had some interest) because, of course, she is not to be trusted. She writes lengthy anecdotal records and case-history forms for the guidance counselors. But she will not write a letter of protest or even sign a petition. Teachers conform, within limits, on the side of the majority, because they fear the social consequences of saying no.

Although she complains and suffers, the teacher feels quite at home with an authoritarian principal. A weak principal upsets her. She does not know where she stands. She begins to join small negative groups of her peers. The tension is enormous. When everyone is suffering at the hands of some comma-counting dictator, she does not feel personally persecuted and will accept the most denigrating contempt as only her fair share of the injustice. But when the weak man is inconsistent, she is in torment. She crawls and whines and curries favor ruthlessly. When the ax shaves the neck (it never really decapitates regulars—only substitutes) of a colleague, she feels the strong relief and pleasure that people feel in battle or on highways when somebody else—*not me!*—gets killed.

The children are the enemy and she fears them. She cannot be aggressive and angry with supervisors or fellow teachers, so the children are fair game. Of course she has ways of working with them: she is not always in a rage. She uses fear, seduction, guilt, concern, and love. She uses threats and sarcasm and rejection.

She cannot abide the children who are most like her. If she is passive, dependent, guilt-ridden, lacking confidence, she will be infuriated by the passive, failure-prone, meek, fearful child. If she is "strong," willful, assertive, rigid, she will be enraged by the willful, assertive kids who stand up to her, who question her wisdom or sincerity or authority. She will bully the weakest child in the hope that the strongest child will be intimidated. She will encourage the class to scapegoat a classmate, in the hope that the class will not scapegoat her.

She is concerned with forms and masks. How can children respect you if you are open and honest with them? How can you control a class in June, the month of heat and relaxation and letdown, if you tell the children what you knew in mid-May: who will be held over? Let the anxious ones sweat it out.

You must have rationalizations for your failures—administration or race or parents or last year's teacher or books-and-supplies. You must have rationalizations for your lack of imagination and energy: "busywork." Busywork—copying four lines of a math problem when the answer is one number which can be worked out in one's head; training in being careful and thorough, in penmanship, in thinking, in anything but what it is: training in sterility and conformity, while the teacher catches up on clerical work. And above all, you must train the children well: books and knowledge are not a reward, they are a punishment. Arts and crafts are the rewards for a good day. Gym is the reward. Never the WORD!

I have a vision of the New York City school system today. At the top: tough, authoritarian, political Irish Catholics who send their children to parochial school and despise the teachers and the children who don't have the guts or the money to get out. In the middle: teachers and school supervisors, who have come from lower-class white minorities, many of them (like the Italians and the Jews) strongly marked by cultural masochism. And at the bottom: the children. Is it so different elsewhere?

In general, the system is certainly one of the most secure and protected of all the secure and protected government jobs. It is, to judge by its personnel, quite adequately paid and vacationed and pensioned.

But it is a medieval serfdom and the serfs are willing and compliant participants. They complain and dissipate their energies in complaining. They hate and dissipate their hatred in suffering, in provoking guilt, in destroying the children around them. Then they stand over the corpses weeping, weeping at the terrible system, this devil machine, this THING that did it, that did it to THEM, that did not let them succeed. They drive with a passionate overpowering drive toward failure and in this, at least and overwhelmingly, they succeed.

And don't tell me they don't fail with the middle-class children too, only the failure is one of mind and imagination and openness and courage, not the paper skills of math concepts and reading levels.

Saul Alinsky, the organizer, says a democracy lacking in popular participation dies of paralysis. But participation requires strength and courage and faith and love. The school system, lacking these, dies of paralysis every day.

Maybe what the teachers of the immigrants of fifty years ago had was not better children in a more mobile society. The babies out of Italy with the evil eye and the garlic charm around the neck were surely as "disadvantaged," culturally and economically, as the Puerto Rican or Negro children today. Maybe what the teachers had then was more courage, more self-respect, and a fair share of faith in their jobs and themselves and their children.

When I showed these pages to other teachers, they invariably remarked, "It's so true—about them." At first I was amused by their insistence on excluding themselves. But that was precisely my own reaction too. I was so sure that I was not one of the teachers I had described. It became uncomfortably clear that I could not condemn other teachers for their blindness as long as I too was blind. And when I returned to the log, reluctantly I began to discover how much a part of the world of teachers I was.

MATH

We've been reviewing the math laws, using the Cuisinaire Rods. Now I show them again how the laws applied to multiplication. Kids are funny. You work things through with them a dozen times, and all of a sudden the bits and pieces fall into place for them and there they are—Columbus discovering America all over again.

"Oh sweat!" they murmur in the tones of awe and reverence of a nun viewing Chartres for the first time.

And then some of them will be all caught up in the process and the excitement of mastery and will work problems through for an hour, two hours straight, and come and ask you for homework besides.

LUIS

I sent Luis to get the mail in the office, knowing that there was an envelope in my box addressed to him. It was a pamphlet on cactus plants which we had sent away for. He did not read the label. When I pointed it out, he held it delicately, read his name and the return address, turned it this way and that, with diffidence let others see it. It was many minutes before he opened it very gently and carefully. Then he and Roberto went off to a corner to make a lengthy exploration of its contents.

SHELLEY

Shelley, the quiet one, was listening to Pete Seeger through the head phones on the tape recorder. She suddenly burst into song. She was so beautifully unaware of her involvement that we had to explain to her why the class had exploded in friendly laughter.

2

FREEDOM

The world of the teacher is not the world of children. Because there are so many children around it is easy for adults not to recognize this fact. After a while, many children seem to forget it too.

From the beginning of my teaching, I resented the cool authoritarian atmosphere of many classrooms, the tedium, the restraint. I tended to be permissive, to a large extent because I did not know how to be anything else. What I did out of weakness I justified in terms of a loose and sentimental psychology.

But even when I learned to run a relatively tight classroom, I was still uncomfortable. What teachers were expected to teach, and the methodology prescribed, seemed dull, illogical, and unnecessarily punishing to little children. Dewey, in the public schools, had been reduced to committee work and even that was largely limited to the social studies. The post-Sputnik furor and the rage of the black community at the failure of education in their schools produced what seemed to me a negative reaction: an increased emphasis on all that was deadly and constricting in the curriculum and the classroom. And children did not stop failing.

The All-Day Neighborhood Schools program, in which I worked for a year and which attempted to bring the schools closer to the community, was humane in intent and practice, but it made little difference in the children's learning to read. The descriptions of Summerhill were attractive for a while but they were disturbing too. The idea of total freedom, of complete lack of restraint and "discipline," did not seem workable, certainly not in a day school setting where the children not only were vulnerable, as I was, to pressures within the school, but from which they returned each night to an environment whose standards of behavior were totally different. Besides, I sensed an antiintellectualism in Summerhill which I could not accept.

The English experiments in the primary schools were much more exciting. Returning to Dewey, but this time armed with the writings of Piaget, English educators had been reforming their schools in what seemed to be radical ways. Freedom, in the English classroom, was combined with a stimulating emphasis on learning. Trusting the children, the educators provided them with both the materials and the environment in which a child, in a child's way, could follow his own needs and interests and *learn*. The teacher was no longer the orchestra leader rapping out silence or appropriate responses on command. Instead the teacher became the helping adult, guiding and supporting the little children as they explored their world, helping them when and if they needed help. The underlying assumption was that children, by all the evidence from their moment of birth, wanted to learn and could not help learning, and that the school's role was to facilitate rather than destroy this natural impulse.

The concept of the "integrated day" or the "open classroom," as the English experiments were called, was also satisfying to me emotionally. Discipline as a problem would of course disappear in a classroom in which children were too busy to be bad, too engrossed to be bored, too free to be sulky and hostile.

Around this time, I had escaped from the marine drill of a middle-class school to an experimental school in East Harlem. At the end of my first year there, I concluded that most of the experimental changes were really administrative ones, as usual responses more to adults' needs than to children's, and the following school year I set out to operate my class according to the English model.

One experimental change that the school had instituted was to group children heterogeneously by age and grade rather than by tested ability, as was the general practice. This proved to be the most difficult change for teachers to accept. The twenty-two children in my class ranged in ability and performance from bottom to top, a spread of as much as eight years in one fifth-grade class. Supervisors encouraged teachers to do as much grouping within the class as possible. Even classes set up by ability often would need two or three groups, with different lessons for each group, in order to "meet the children's needs." In a class where the range was so great, such grouping was difficult and inadequate. But teachers and supervisors resisted the idea of complete individualization of instruction, both because the idea was alien and therefore threatening, and because we were not equipped with the books and voluminous materials that would be necessary.

Indeed, in my fifth-grade class, we had few materials to explore and manipulate and very few library books. Sets of texts were provided, all at fifth-grade level, and it was a continuing struggle to extract math books and readers from the lower grades to use with the children who were three or four or five years behind in their skills. The only diagnosis of the children's needs was the inadequate one provided by the city-wide test scores. The tests themselves had been administered the previous April. In addition, the school day was broken into segments as the children went to special reading classes or to gym or had a science or music teacher come to them. It was unusual to have a block of time as long as two hours on any day without some such interruption. All these difficulties stood in the way of what I wanted to do.

There were, besides, no reassuring books of instructions on how-to-set-up a free and open classroom English style. The English educators, with alarming consistency, included the free teacher in the free classroom. While there were descriptions of various classes available in the press, the basic assumption seemed to be that each teacher must learn to be free in her own classroom in her own way. The minute you had a methodology set down you obviously had betrayed the whole idea.

But in desperation I determined to explore the possibilities of a freer classroom in my fifth grade. I was confronted by twenty-two children, all but three of them black or Puerto Rican. They had come to me from middle-income co-ops, from low-income housing, and from the transient population of the tenements. Some could not read at all; almost half had been held over on grade at some time in the past. Some had very little English at their command. And some had severe enough physical or emotional problems as to require extensive help, which was not of course available.

I did not have a clear plan for what I wanted to do. To my supervisors I described it as "an attempt to meet the challenge of the heterogeneous class," jargon which was less threatening to them than a more accurate description would have been. They had not heard of the English schools experiments in any case, and they were under pressure to produce such results as were measurable on reading tests. Beyond that goal, they had little interest. They were convinced, though, that the "experimental school" that they were running, if given enough time, would prove a success. What a teacher did behind closed doors was a matter of her "teaching style" and the supervisors's concern was only to hope that it would be successful, no matter what it was.

Within these limitations I was determined to work. School opening had been delayed by the short strike of 1967. But the children arrived, in spite of the delay, with their September manners, quiet, observant, taking the measure of their new teacher. They found desks for themselves, into which they proudly stuffed the evidence of their good intentions, new notebooks and pencils and rulers and crayons.

I tried to explain my hopes for the class, saying that I would let them choose what they wanted to study as much as possible. But they found the idea incomprehensible, or, if not that, then incredible. I laid out what materials I had on tables and shelves and in unlocked closets: my own set of Cuisinaire Number Rods, some toys and games, books, scales, whatnot—everything except art supplies. I justified the exclusion of the latter on the grounds that "art" was always the escape activity in school: "If you are good now, you may paint or draw later." I was sure that the children would never choose the academic options if art were a choice. Although I was aware of my prejudices, I was also aware of the supervisors's. In a test-oriented school, I lacked the courage to put this matter to a test. There would be opportunities later on for the children to "have art," as a gift if not an option.

I invited the children to wander about the room to investigate the materials. They were still in the throes of first-week-of-school good manners. Most of the children sat at their desks playing with the Cuisinaire Rods, building airy towers and squat enclosed forts, or, surprisingly, using them as they would crayons, to lay out a flat picture of a house with a pitched roof and chimney. Only a few walked around, and they did not open closet doors nor poke around on shelves. They walked almost on tiptoe, like intruders not sure how to extricate themselves from an embarrassing situation. Maybe they did not understand the reason for the invitation and did not trust it. They did not know what was expected and played it safe. Or else they settled for the first attraction, plunging into the doing right away.

I noted in my log that Jose, fresh from parochial school, sat quietly looking around, doing nothing. Only in rereading this entry did I realize that even I, recording the event, equated "looking around" with doing nothing.

In those first days, most of the children saw freedom as "freedom to play." Number rods became toys. Spring scales became weapons, from which clumsy objects could be launched with gratifying noise. The numbers on the scales were ignored. Balance beams, which I previously had made for another class, held the same destructive fascination that toy makers capitalize on: the beams were loaded with infinite patience until they reached the reckless moment when the whole thing came crashing down. When I insisted that the children record their observations and experiments, trying to legitimize their activity, the most avid balancers lost all interest. Sea shells became improvised templates to be used in the dull inaccurate pattern drawings they rarely seemed to tire of or go beyond.

I never came to terms that year, or in the years following, with their need to play and with their seeming inability to play constructively and creatively. I did not (and do not) know how to make use of their playing. I did not trust them enough to wait while they exhausted the possibilities of the materials out of their needs and experience. Often the materials were lost or destroyed long before they had explored them fully. And I could not wait to see if they would go further with the materials by themselves. I was not able to help them find new meanings in the materials, not beyond the prosaic academic tasks I tried to impose too soon upon them.

Their play, indeed, became for me not an expression of freedom but an obstacle to it. So from the beginning I began defining freedom for them, only half aware that definition was, automatically, denial.

Thus, not believing in what I wanted as a teacher most desperately to believe, I decided that we must inch our way to freedom. Certain times of the day would be set aside as free time. When the children took me literally, choosing to play or talk even in this limited free time, I backed down further. Like colonials or slaves, they were not ready for freedom. Therefore clearly defined and carefully structured tasks must be provided for them. I did not dare experiment with real freedom of choice and action although it was a long time before I could admit this to myself. The admission was not a liberating one. It served instead more to help me excuse my limitations and tolerate the limitations under which teachers work than it did to strengthen my resolve to go forward to freedom.

The children too were in strange territory. They clung to their turf. The idea of moving from one place to another to work at specific jobs was acceptable. But the notion that there need not be a home base from which they departed, a desk which was theirs, seemed to make them uncomfortable. They wanted a defined place to go when they entered the room, when they finished a job, when they were acting as a group. They wanted to pick their neighbors if they could and to stay with them.

Even the business of lining up was difficult. Standard procedure is to line up according to size. A vote showed that the majority of the children did not like lining up by size. But when we practiced complete freedom in lining up, the result was weeks of bickering and bullying. The worst problems were solved by rotating the job of line leader. Eventually they got bored with arguing about position and came to accept the random lineup. But what a long and noisy time it was! And when a new child joined the class, or when another teacher or an aide was in charge, there was always an outbreak of disorder, as children tried to explain the system to people unfamiliar with it and unwilling to accept it.

As to their ideas about appropriate classroom behavior, when I asked for them, they suggested staying in your seat, raising your hand if you wanted to talk or get something or take a drink. At least in the beginning they did not trust my words but voiced, with the brilliant intuition of children, the message of my emotions.

Not that they stayed in their seats or raised their hands. Within days, the stark advice appeared in my log: Isolate George, Julio, Walter, Carl.

There will always be a George, a Julio, a Walter, a Carl. They have not been school broken. They have problems with reading and math. They have problems with being people. They are bored, foolish, hypertense, restless, angry. They do not know what to do with themselves, but they do not want you to tell them what to do. I was convinced that even these children would see the new freedom in the classroom as a great gift which they had always wanted, in whose absence school was an intolerable burden and punishment. What I

Freedom

really wanted was for them to be civilized and constructive and cooperative—to be good.

They were not about to see things in my terms. For some of the children, the "good" ones, freedom to choose was part of some game whose rules and limits had simply not yet been defined. They tested uneasily to find out what the limits were. For some, freedom meant that now they would be able to draw all day, and of course they were quickly set straight on that score. But the boys who needed isolation had always had "freedom" in school, because they had always behaved according to their own internal needs.

They had never really enjoyed the freedom. They had always, accurately, seen it as a rejection. You let me do what I want because you can't control me. You can't make me BE GOOD. This can only mean that you find me uncontrollably BAD. Therefore freedom is bad. In the past they had made deals, bargaining, consciously or not, with their teachers. If you let me do this, I will be good (*i.e.*, quiet) for x numbers of minutes. If you do not let me do that, I will have a tantrum or will curse or throw chairs or get in a fight. Each year they had to discover, by trial and error, what the acceptable terms were.

And each year, in the first months of exploratory turmoil, George, Julio, Walter, Carl remember wistfully that last year they were "good." They accuse you of incompetence and indifference because you have not yet discovered how to make them be good. They want to be good but they are convinced that they have no control over their own behavior. They can only maneuver and bargain and malfunction until *you* finally discover the formula (of fear or seduction) that will impose upon them the behavior that they insist they value highly. They believe in original sin, and everything they do seems to reinforce their belief in their innate wickedness. Their actions seem to plead for you to produce some miraculous redemption in whose permanence they do not really have any faith at all.

Now and then we had a class discussion of behavior. For teachers, such classroom discussions are often a form of self-indulgence which is highly approved by guidance counselors. In the course of the discussion children supposedly will discover profoundly useful insights into their motivation and behavior. To some extent this happens. But I discovered, in retrospect, that my choice of the "teachable moment" was determined more by my needs than by the children's. When the class had affronted me beyond bearing, it was almost enjoyable to set the hour's duties aside and "have a discussion."

The children, predictably, would parrot all the expected rules and rituals of behavior as though they had just discovered them. Asked for help in determining what the consequences of disruption should be, they would come up with the harshest of punishments: hit him with a ruler, send him to Mr. Whoever-had the-meanest-reputation-in-the-school, stand him in the corner leaning on his fingertips, don't let him sit all day, call his mother so she'll give him a beating.

At first I concluded that they had been exposed to all kinds of sadism in the past. But their descriptions were tinged to some extent by fantasy. Usually the most disruptive children had the most punitive suggestions. They were also the ones most likely to describe appropriate behavior in impossibly repressive terms.

However enjoyable it initially was for me as the suffering adult to listen to their breast beating, sooner or later I would be oppressed by the tenor of the discussions.

In one such discussion, they as usual defined good behavior in the most puritanical school terms: always busy, always quiet, always still. Anything else, by definition, was bad. So I asked them if they could think of any good ways to be bad. After all, sometimes you needed some release from an unbearable task or tension.

They settled on three possibilities to start with.
You could stop working, do nothing at all, daydream.
You could walk to the sink, wash up, clean the sink, take a drink.
You could go and look out of the window for a while.

Windows in classrooms are designed so that the child at his low

Freedom

desk can see little of the world outside. This is surely deliberate. How rarely children, or teachers for that matter, seem to be aware of windows. It is as if, upon entering the school, one sets the environment securely and firmly aside, not only symbolically but intellectually and physically. One concentrates all one's attention inward, inside the walls. It is part of the jail psychology that one develops in the schools. Activity and excitement are provided, if at all, by the life in the corridors, almost never by the streets outside.

It was literally years before I even became aware of the wall that windows are. Windows were there to have pictures pasted on or to be raised or lowered the mandatory six inches. That I developed, at home, a strong resistance to drawing curtains and pulling down shades, even at night, had for me no connection with the fact that I worked in a spiritually blind room every day. When an astute if insensitive architect in New York City went the logical step to designing a school without any windows, I was outraged but for no sensible reason I could think of at the time.

Looking out of windows was, at any rate, institutionalized in our room as a good way to be bad.

Within a day or two I noticed that Walter was unusually restless. He wasn't fighting or throwing things, but he was walking, walking, walking. He made frequent trips to the sink. With sidelong glances, he made long detours to the window, where he would drape himself dramatically on the sill, nose pointed to the glass but eyes seeking me out.

He knew. Time and again I would tell him, impatiently, to sit down, to stop wandering. He was testing me, but he knew I would fail. Finally, one day, he confronted me angrily with my failure.

All I could do was admit he was right. The new rules and ways were unfamiliar to me too. After years of teaching I too had learned to internalize the school definitions of good/bad. He must try to be be patient with me when I failed and to remind me when I forgot. I in turn would try to be patient with him. He was not to be placated so easily. The science teacher was due in and he was all primed for battle. I told him that he was angry with me, after all, and not with the science teacher, at least not yet. If he could set aside his anger during science, he was quite welcome to resume the business of being mad at me when I returned to the room. He managed to suppress most of a smile of satisfaction, and after science he graciously and pointedly declined to be angry.

Time and again the children and I were to go through such incidents and time and again we failed one another. I was all too willing to attribute their failure to their years of authoritarian schooling. It was not until I returned to the log after the school year had ended that I even began to be aware of the degree to which I was, subtly or stridently, denying the freedom that I was so sure I wanted and that, at the time, I was so sure the children were not ready for.

PUPIL ROUTINES AND REQUIREMENTS

2.4 *Indoor Lineup*

    2.4.1 Grades 3 through 6 line up in the lunchroom by class. No talking is permitted.

    2.4.2 Grades 1 and 2 are seated by class in the auditorium. No talking is permitted.

3 *Going Up to Classroom*

Pupils move quickly and silently up to class under supervision of the class teacher.

4 *In the Classroom*

    4.1 Every pupil should be assigned a permanent clothing hook.

    4.2 The teacher established and consistently carries out routines for hanging and getting clothing.

    4.3 All pupils (unless written exclusion signed by parent)

Freedom

participate respectfully in opening exercises, led by pupil, every morning except assembly days.

4.4 During recitation lessons, pupils should raise hands to indicate desire to make a contribution, encouraged to speak in full sentences.

4.5 *Leaving the Room*

    4.5.1 Pupil must ask for permission to go to bathroom.

    4.5.2 A notation in the "Out-of-Room" book must be made for every child leaving a room for any reason (except pre-K, K, and 1st grade). (Notation must include: date; child's name; destination; time leaving; time returned).

    4.5.3 No pupil leaves a room without a room pass.

    4.5.5 *Bathroom Hours*

    Unless an emergency, bathrooms may *not* be used before 10:00 a.m. (except pre-K, K, and 1st grade).

4.7 *Eating Candy, Cookies, etc.*

Eating of any kind is forbidden in any part of the building other than the lunchroom except for specifically planned social activities and/or special curriculum experiences in the classroom.

4.8 Gum chewing is forbidden anywhere in the school building. (The teacher *must* set the example.)

6.11.2 NOT PERMITTED AT ANY TIME: (in playground)
1. Taking any food out of lunchroom.
2. Running—unless part of an organized game.
3. Climbing fences.
4. Jumping on benches.
5. Wrestling or other horseplay.
6. Leaving yard for home, street, stores.
7. Leaving assigned play area.

7. *Care of Books, Materials, etc.*
   7.1 Care of and respect for books, etc., is essential for many reasons.
   1. *EVERY* BOOK IN A CHILD'S CARE SHOULD BE COVERED AT ALL TIMES.
   2. Scribbling, doodling, drawing in notebooks should be prevented and discouraged.
   4. Pupils should empty their desks regularly under the routine supervision of the teacher and everything other than approved books and materials should be discarded on the spot or taken home at 3:00.

(These excerpts from *Staff bulletin*, January 31, 1968, are printed as they appeared.)

GOING TO THE BATHROOM

It seems so simple. If someone has to go let him go. But there are conflicts. School policy is that children should not go before ten a.m. and before two in the afternoon. Except In An Extreme Emergency.

Bathroom has always been the refuge for bored children. They make appointments with their friends. Children come past the door and give the high sign and off they go. Or some children, the unnaturally quiet ones, like Belinda, who never ever permit themselves release inside the room, will depart for ten minutes of joyous freedom once or twice a day. (Bathroom: the individualized recess?) For some children the start of a new lesson is somehow a stimulus for which the bathroom trip is the conditioned response.

3

PLANNING, TEACHING, LEARNING

By trial and error I worked out a program that was at least a beginning toward my amorphous goal of a free classroom.

I planned two or three lessons daily that could include most or all of the class. I might read a story to the class or have discussions on general topics that came up, or present a film on science. Or there might be lessons on spelling patterns or explorations of language—syntax and dialect—or expositions in math. For although the children varied greatly in their mastery of the skills, they almost all shared a profound and unquestioning ignorance about what math *meant*. Even those who could perform the functions impeccably had almost no insight into the processes themselves.

In addition, I would provide a list of independent activities in several areas. These the children might pursue alone, with a buddy, or in a group. The activities were listed with no identification as to their level of difficulty. Children knew which they could do or which they were strong enough to attempt. There were always included on the list some tasks which were drill or dull, like alphabetizing, penmanship, multiplication facts. Children picked these sometimes because they could succeed at them or because they needed a clearly defined and limited task which made minimal demands of them. In the same way, a housewife might take a break in the day's chores and turn to mending socks or rearranging bureau drawers. As time went by they tended to ignore most of these choices, although some turned the math drills into a competitive game that gathered popularity as they increased their skill, until by the end of the year it was a favorite pastime.

Fairly often I would include one task for which they were all responsible, although each child could decide when during his day to do it. This practice helped those children who compulsively settled on one kind of task for weeks at a time, or those who, whether from fear or inadequacy, would always avoid certain kinds of tasks, or those who simply did not know where to begin when faced with "too many" choices.

In a short time children began to make suggestions of their own for the list. Eventually a number of children freed themselves from the list entirely, even asking to be excused from the whole-class lessons in order to pursue their own work.

On the negative side there were always some children I could not reach. Either because of blind spots in me or in them we never met, or only rarely, on the road to learning. Often I failed to take advantage of the signals they gave me, either because of my own academic prejudices or because I did not understand them until it was too late.

As the months passed, I found it easier and easier to schedule individual conferences or small group lessons. The children, who resisted grouping because to them it meant visible evidence of inferiority, gradually became more willing participants. One thing that helped was that I eventually learned to permit children the right to refuse the group lesson, no matter how it pained me. Besides, group activities were often fun, combining social pleasures with challenging games and resulting in successful learning. Often children competent in the topic to be taught would ask to be included, further blurring the lines that the selected children resented.

As for materials, there were either too many or never enough. I tended to rely on the materials to illuminate the lessons. I was thus constantly being taken by surprise by complexities and inadequacies in the materials or in my presentation. Lessons never seemed to come in small enough steps. Children had the oddest notions and misconceptions. No matter how simple and specialized the materials, they were never controlled and specific enough to meet everyone's needs, so that unexpected variables would be introduced to throw us off.

In a simple counting task, using beans, a child announced firmly that he could go no further. "Run out of beans?" I asked. "Nope. Ran out of numbers." How beautiful and mysterious and finite. After 133, no more numbers!

Or they were busy measuring and making their own rulers. Consider the idea that inches and feet are fixed standards. Annie made a ruler on a running cardboard strip that contained all the numbers from 1 to 12, over and over again, but no two spaces were equal. Much later, when we were keeping plant records, Roberto and another child recorded the height of their tiny plants as two feet instead of two inches.

The children had each abstracted one quality to generalize. Roberto generalized that height can be labeled, but any measuring term would do. Annie generalized that a foot contained twelve numbered spaces, not that the spaces have a fixed and equal dimension.

In a way the very untidiness of our activities helped me to discover their confusions. Number problems on paper, or even, perhaps, a programmed workbook with its built-in protection from any deviation, would not so readily uncover their misconceptions. Add to such built-in blinders the fact that children influence one another, and the problem of uncovering the actual living misconception is seen in its actual proportion. Luisa, seemingly so attentive and serious, tended to use her neighbor's figures and could never explain how a single answer was gotten, whether she really knew or not. Linda "knew" what feet and inches were, but once she started working with Annie her knowledge could not withstand Annie's superior and cavalier self-confidence. In a short while her ruler began to look like Annie's erratic measure.

Besides making the wrong generalizations, the children often had difficulty in making any generalizations at all. This I came to attribute more often to a habit of mind rather than a lack of ability. Children would parrot answers they had memorized. If one foot equaled twelve inches, what would two feet equal? Twenty-four inches. And three feet? Don't know. How did you figure out the number of inches in two feet? My teacher tole me las' year.

In such cases they tended to put down any number as an answer if they thought that the work would not be checked or if they thought that the teacher would prefer the work done any old way rather than not at all. In the latter case, they would be accused of laziness, naturally. Most children seemed not to have considered the possibility that they could tell the teacher they did not know, did not understand, and ask her for clarification. "Don't know" was a technique for avoiding work, not a prerequisite for getting help. It is inconceivable to most children that they have a right to demand teaching on their terms from the teacher. SHE sets the terms and limits for the lessons. If they do not understand what she is teaching them, either they do not know that they do not understand or else they assume that the fault lies in them (they are stupid, uninterested, inattentive, lazy . . .) and that there is nothing they or anyone can do to help them.

In such a climate, how else but by inspection of individual activities over a period of time and in a variety of environments can one discover the misconceptions? Or, as an adult long familiar with such "simple" ideas, discover the complexities involved in such a seemingly commonplace, uncomplicated idea as fixed standard measurement?

A third-grade teacher told me that she no longer used manipulative materials because "they only confuse the children." What she did not recognize was that the confusions were there, hidden by the parrot answers and parrot drills, and that the children revealed their misconceptions or lack of understanding precisely in the way they coped with abstractions concretely. She found unbearable the noise, the disorder, the confusions that go with the use of materials, when the children are not accustomed to working that way. The demand for total silence in the classroom is an administrative one. It is not a prerequisite for learning but quite the opposite. Like so many other teachers indoctrinated in silence, this one felt threatened in its absence. So after each attempt to work with materials, she would return with relief to pencil and paper. If the problems were parceled out in neat doses, most of the children, abstracting a ritual, could work their way through a page. When later they encountered the problem in a different environment and form, it was only to be expected that only a few would "remember." You teach them and teach them and they forget everything they have learned.

So we give them extra homework which older brothers and sisters, or worried parents, obligingly work out for them. Julio's homework, which he turned in with such beaming pride, had all been done by his sister. I accepted it without comment, taking what comfort I could from the knowledge that his sister was doing for him this year what she could not do for herself in my class the year before.

Teachers are under pressure from parents and supervisors to give homework every day. I gave the children homework assignments reluctantly and infrequently, and then usually only in response to supervisors's or parents's complaints. Record keeping was a problem for the children and for me. I found it difficult to keep abreast of their work or to devise appropriate follow-up lessons or to check to see that these, when provided, were done. I knew that I would not be able to check their homework daily to see to its correctness. Merely to check to see that it was done seemed pointless.

Some children always do their homework, some children never do. Carl, supervised by a strict mother, turned out more homework than classwork. John, whose mother checked his work too, was always reliable. Often he turned in extra work, thoughtful little stories that revealed him to me. A bright, polite, and good-natured boy, he tended to be an isolate in class. I began to know him by the quality of his written work because he had chosen, by his silence and isolation, to hide himself from me.

I still have not solved the homework problem. But during that year it gradually faded away. Homework would often consist of a request to complete some of the day's unfinished work. And as time went by more and more children devised their own homework. Shelley liked to take the number rods home and work through assignments. Maria borrowed them too but gave up fairly soon. Her mother wondered why she was using such babyish toys. Some children liked to take math workbooks home and would bring back page after page of completed work. When there was a topic in the air that excited them, like plants and animals, they had an unspoken competition to see who could find the most interesting books on the subject. They exchanged the books and took them home and read them and copied pages from them or drew pictures.

Some children, like Diana and George, just enjoyed taking many books home. They went back and forth, loaded down, and for them the learned voyage was enough to satisfy their homework needs. They had a need to be seen with books, to look like scholars. Carl took home a little bit of everything but he acted under duress and found no joy in it. Seth reduced everything, whenever possible, to one tiny scrap of paper folded over and over into the minutest shape, stuffed it deep in his shirt pocket, stuck a grimy chewed down inch of pencil into his pocket, and usually spent the afternoon in playground or gym, playing basketball. But his homework was almost always done.

The planning that seemed ultimately to work best for me was the planning that took place from day to day as problems were discovered or as interests were expressed. No matter how, each year, I vow to follow the manuals and the curriculum, eventually I find it impossible to do so. Never being provided with a workmanlike diagnosis of the children's stage of learning (the reading and math tests are only the coarsest and most useless of instruments, except for providing statistical overviews, always depressing, of the entire school population), I was always discovering, in April and May, hitherto unnoticed gaps which had to be filled. My periodic attempts to "diagnose" individual children usually disintegrated in a flurry of charts full of an overabundance of unmanageable specifics.

So I tried to keep in mind some simple goals: competence in reading words, some increased understanding and interest in materials read, some pleasure in language, some basic skills in math, an increase in the ability to ask questions and to think, a reawakened delight in learning. Beyond that, I had to trust the children. In the long run and for the majority, the trust was not misplaced.

I concluded, finally, partly in self-defense, that learning could take place without the child having to communicate constantly with the teacher. But I did not think teaching could take place without constant communication with the children—a profound difference, in a school system where somehow people were convinced that they were teaching in spite of all the evidence that children were not learning. The observation left me still strung up on the problem of how to devise and structure a room and a program where learning, if not always teaching, could take place.

THE ARTS AND CRAFTS CREW

Roberto, Luis, and Wilfredo found an arts and crafts book and came to me for permission to construct some of the things in class. My immediate reaction was no. I had to run down, like a litany, all the jargon justifications before I could permit myself to say yes: they would benefit by having to read the instructions and follow them, by having to measure accurately, by having to share a task and complete it. I still felt, and very strongly, that if something is fun it can't be learning.

THE WORLD OF ADULTS

I am on the outs with my supervisors again. Challenging their authority and/or judgments. But we are too professional, aren't we, to argue? And so I notice that my class is singled out for unusual attention. In a noisy assembly, it is my moderately noisy class who is publicly identified for reprimand. Or at lineup time in the yard, I (and my class with me) become invisible. In a lunchroom full of waiting classes but empty of teachers, once again I waited almost five minutes before my presence, yellow sweater and bulk and all, was noticed in the center aisle directly across from the assistant principal at the microphone, directing departures. Eventually he called our class and told us we might go up to our room. The kids notice it. They are prepared, as usual, to blame themselves. I explain that it is not their fault, that I had managed to earn the supervisors' disapproval. I point out that as a result we are more noticeable than usual and that we should all—they and I—toe the line more scrupulously for a while. They are very interested in this evidence that adults behave in real ways, like kids. They know it anyway but they usually pretend, in school, that the adults are exempt from humanity.

4

ON-THE-JOB TRAINING

I wanted, but I did not trust, freedom for myself and for my children. The one attitude that is basic to the operation of the schools is distrust. All the rules and regulations, most of the prescriptions for curriculum and the pedegogical strategies devised have their roots in distrust, although of course they are verdantly justified by all kinds of reasonable explanations.

As a student and then as a teacher I accepted the encrusted rules without really questioning most of them. Of course it makes sense to line up children, to march them silently, to insist on total silence when they assemble in the auditorium, to forbid them to eat candy or chew gum in class, to follow routines for hanging up coats or taking drinks or going to the bathroom.

At the beach, teen-agers, full of potential violence, line up for drinks at the fountains on the boardwalk and patiently wait their turn. Is it because they have internalized the school patterns so completely? But then why have they not been able to do so within the schools themselves?

The little savages of *The Lord of the Flies* were *school* children. Certainly the author saw children as pupils. The parable makes no sense otherwise.

School rules speak to the felt need as seen by the adults. But much more do they speak to the expectation than any privilege will be abused, that the only alternative to mandatory silence is noise, the only possible consequence of freedom, chaos and savagery.

At any rate it was difficult to divest myself of the rituals and the rationalizations for them. In consequence, in the first months we had many unnecessary confrontations. I had thought that in trying to piece together the jigsaw of my own life, I had learned not to discard the troublesome pieces that would not fit, but to keep rearranging the patterns until everything finally made sense. In the classroom, working with a somewhat different kind of puzzle, I was again trying to find the pattern. But I did not have a zealot's convictions to sustain me. I was vulnerable to demands and criticisms from others who either did not understand or did not support my ideas or who were openly hostile to them. To some extent I set aside those misfitting attitudes in myself which interfered with my "plans" (but which pacified supervisors) and concentrated on those of the children who still continued to resist me. Thus, while I was trying to understand what was going on, I had unconsciously narrowed my view so that a large part of myself was safely hidden.

Our lessons with the whole class were unpredictable. Often the group was unruly. Some teachers have learned how to wait out the restlessness; but when I tried to do it, feeling insecure in the procedure, I tended to wait too long, setting impossible—but ultimately attainable—standards of quiet "attention." Where in the beginning a handful were slow in coming to order, eventually in the course of waiting them out first one and then another would have his moments of wiggling and fussing. Only the good good good sat serenely throughout, their patience an unintended rebuke, their stillness the result of years of practice. But I could not give up the conviction—or the prejudice—that it was important that the whole class learn to sit in silence, accepting a single lesson directed at all of them at the same time.

Two years later, confronting a completely different kind of class straight out of *Lord of the Flies*, I finally saw the whole-class lesson for what it was.

In the midst of a lesson of small consequence and content, presented after weeks of struggle to achieve some order out of inherited chaos, I became aware of what was really happening. I was not giving a lesson to the whole class at all. The class, from exhaustion or compassion, was prepared to give me silence while I conducted a series of two- or three-minute individual lessons, over and over and over, with a series of children selected at random from a bored inattentive and, for the moment, unresisting mass. It was and is the most inefficient and irritating way to teach. The illusion of efficiency, of mass-production instruction, is shattered as child after child demonstrates that all he has been doing has been waiting patiently for the lesson to be over, or at best for his turn when the teacher would give him a three-minute lesson individually tailored to his revealed needs.

It turns out in practice that the only times one really needs the participation of the whole group are those occasions when announcements must be made or a matter of common interest is to be discussed or when the children must be prepared for a fire drill or other orderly departure. But it is hard for the teacher to accept the seeming inefficiency of individualization and repetition.

I will grant that without an abundance of materials and books the children must rely heavily on the teacher for the explanations and information which they could, in most instances, get for themselves or from one another. But teachers continue to feel that it would be much more efficient (how the factory word keeps recurring!) if all the little machines could be turned on and off simultaneously, their little gears meshing in unison, their output predictable and prompt.

But they often refused to accept synchronization. In the log I put it all on the children. When would they develop a sense of group responsibility? No one person was very bad, but there were many low-level chatterers and nonconformists. They took just a little longer to respond, to begin or to end things. They managed to be a little different from the others in the performance of a task. For instance, writing seventeen numbers on one side of a spelling paper and thirteen on the other instead of fifteen on each. I felt it was inconsistent to insist on a particular order but I insisted anyway. And I managed, reasonably, to justify my insistence.

Observing the nonconformists, I tried to understand why they found it so hard to surrender completely in the smallest, most unimportant matters. (I was not then considering why I found it so difficult too.)

They did not resist conforming out of principle, out of a feeling that such comma-counting demands were demeaning and nonsensical. They seemed to see compliance as surrender, as evidence that they were weak.

And they are weak. They cannot handle freedom and they cannot handle the lack of it. Freedom is a threat. It indulges them in their own egocentric fantasies of infinite wickedness. Why are you turning the monster inside loose upon an unsuspecting world?

The result is a kind of paradox. They hate, they claim, a rigid structure and an orderly routine. Day in day out they resist, fighting the same idiotic battles over and over again. They do not learn to accept the structure, to internalize it, or to make a truce with it. They know what to expect when they refuse to conform to it. In the continuing battles with authority they lose, again and again. But they win by losing. They find that the teacher is mean, that she picks on them, that she persecutes them unmercifully. They find that it is all HER fault that they cannot learn. She makes them so miserable and angry that they can't learn. Now there is someone outside themselves to blame for their failure and hard times. So they do not need to risk freedom, risk handling their own lives themselves, risk the act of learning.

This takes the edge off their other unbearable piece of knowledge about themselves, their conviction that they are full of uncontrollable wickedness. The devil outside is always more comfortable to live with than the devil within. You cannot change the teacher. You are absolved from the need to change yourself. Freedom means, even to children who cannot put the thought into words, accountability and responsibility for one's own actions. Freedom means not only making choices but accepting the consequences of those choices. Who will we blame for what we do when we have chosen for ourselves?

Although I was not prepared to pursue the thought and rephrase the arguments in terms of the teacher (distrust, blame-sharing, avoidance of accountability, refusal to come to terms with the children's psychic and physical needs), I was not prepared to give up on the children. The knowledge that the children who could not yet function with freedom could not (like me) function any better with rigid authority was comforting, but only to a small degree. But that knowledge at least prevented me from giving up, even when everything seemed to be going wrong.

There has to be an act of faith in the whole process. There has to be faith that chaos will give way to order, that abrasive quarreling will yield to serenity or at least to some calmer ways of coping with one another's differences. No matter, I told myself, that the class had come to me (not adding, *and I to it*) after years of negative school experiences: the failures, the anger, the boredom, the fragmented views of the world, the inability to think or to permit oneself to be interested, to ask questions, to admit ignorance or errors, the inability to *take risks*. No matter. I had the necessary faith.

I was so sure that I was taking risks, if I thought about my role at all. And to a considerable but unimportant degree I was. I was bucking supervisors on methodology, on curriculum, on planning, on discipline, on homework, on bulletin boards, on gum chewing. What saved me from the full weight of their displeasure at that time was perhaps their perception that I was not as radical as I thought I was. Besides, unsure of my directions I did not ask them to commit themselves in support of me, to share responsibility for my results. ("Feel free," one of the supervisors said, smiling, his voice trailing off into silence, the unspoken ending ringing loudly in the silence between us. Feel free to fail. You'll come around to our way, sooner or later. Feel free to fail.)

Moreover, as far as the supervisors were concerned, my problem children somehow tended after a while to be smaller problems, not drawing as much blood per capita per annum as some other teachers' problems. Besides, I was rarely absent, I handed in my reports on time, and what turmoil I had almost never spilled over into the corridors.

But I continued to be unnerved by the butterflies and the frogs, flitting and leaping about, never settling down, never seeming to do anything. How much better I would have felt about them if they hid themselves from my awareness by sitting quietly, pretending to be good, pretending to be learning. Then I could have ignored them with a clear conscience and paid attention to the others who needed me. But I was in conflict over the noisy room with children wandering about most blatantly uninvolved. What would a parent or a supervisor say?

Besides a teacher must teach. I wanted to settle down with a child or a group and teach them. I wanted to control, direct, explain, clarify, select. But for a long time I had to force myself to be a wanderer too, yielding to children's definitions of an activity.

The children somehow managed to teach me to break away from some habitual responses. Richard brought in a microscope and I permitted the children to go, one or two at a time, to examine it with him. Roberto and his arts and crafts crew wanted to make a witch. Hating myself for indulging them, I said yes, provided they could read the instructions in the crafts book to me. They groaned but they found themselves a good reader to help them with the hard words.

I set up a math game. What attracted the children was the provision of a stack of white paper and brand new sharpened pencils. They promptly discarded my rules as too difficult but they played their own simplified version seriously and quietly for three-quarters of an hour. (Their version remained the one they played.)

I started reading them a story and some children said they had heard it before so could they please read their own books? Only a small struggle this time before I agreed. What had been a situation fraught with possibilities of uproar, as children got bored or as they jockeyed for place in order to better see the pictures, suddenly was transformed into a peaceful and intimate experience, full of pleasure for us all.

On a weekend visit to a park along the Hudson, I had picked up some moss and rotted sticks with fungus attached and best of all a puffball which, when poked, emitted a dark and wonderful cloud of spores. We put them all into a terrarium. The arts and crafts boys, Roberto, Luis, Freddy, were entranced. They hovered over the glass case, talking and watching. They became quite possessive about it, daily making new discoveries about its complex and changing life. They asked question after question. Their first experience with the puffball's magic sent them to the encyclopedia to look up fungus and mushroom. Their reading skills were totally inadequate to cope with the encyclopedia, but they could locate the subjects they were interested in. Their explorations were cursory. They found the variety in the pictures satisfying. But sometimes a picture was too intriguing to be passed over. At last they came to me to ask me to read "about that picture."

I suppose the experience of breaking up into small groups when I read them stories I had selected prepared me and them for the next step. The idea that the teacher could find time during the day to sit and read to them a text which they could not read for themselves but which they could understand and discuss was initially very strange. It was, after all, a reversal of roles. They were defining the lesson and the teacher was in effect doing their bidding. But they very quickly learned to relax and to expect the service. They drew other children into the circle of their enthusiasm and interest. And when they found me too busy to perform they made their own arrangements with a good reader in the class, judging with considerable shrewdness which child could read which level of difficult text.

Sometimes things went so well that I almost felt as though I must be doing something wrong—and I was, in terms of standard operating procedures. I did not examine the good days carefully enough to be able to duplicate them at will. There was always an element of chance involved. Periodically I would still succumb to the pressures of the system, real or imagined, and destroy the rhythm of the class with arbitrary decisions and arbitrary formality. On a Friday, after an unsettled week, I ran the class as a unit the whole day. As usual there were seven or eight nonparticipants, jittery, not functioning, slow to respond, interrupting, quarrelsome, exhausting. It was not the only time I worked that way. Of course not every unit day was as disastrous. But the bad days, somehow, were much easier to duplicate than the beautiful days.

It was not easy to unlearn old ways, especially when much of what one had learned was now safely and solidly lodged deep in one's unconscious mind.

TEACHERS

The cluster teacher decided to try teaching a group in the room while I worked with the other children. In the midst of it an aide entered, unannounced, to check the children's height and weight.

The noise level was high. I found it all tense and unsettling. I am learning not to look at my class through the eyes of visitors. Invariably we look awful to me. My vision suffers marked distortions when it passes through the imagined eye of a stranger.

But I still have not learned to accept fellow teachers tranquilly. They are all too ready to be helpful, that is, critical, explaining why they had problems with my children: obviously I had not trained the children properly, established routines and standards. I spoiled them. I gave them too much freedom. When the children gave evidence of learning and progressing, they would react with insulting astonishment. They reject out of hand that a certain attitude or atmosphere might really be good for children. Of course they can't explain why Carl isn't climbing the walls as much, why Walter hasn't had a fight in weeks and seems to be settling down to work. Happily Julio continues to clown and to irritate other teachers. He supports their dogmas. All the other children become the acceptably inexplicable exceptions which prove their rules.

LITTLE BOXES

Life in school is carefully compartmentalized. There is the box of the classroom with its smaller boxes for gym and cluster teachers and library. There is the box of staff relations, with smaller boxes inside for different grades and groupings. There are the authority boxes, supervisory and union, and it is becoming increasingly difficult to tell them apart. There are the boxes of relations with custodians, school aides and paraprofessionals, parents, community people, and other such lesser forms of life.

There does not seem to be any easy way to open up the little boxes to one another. We are always popping out, grinning like any other jacks-in-the-box, and getting our heads banged as we are popped back in. It becomes more comfortable for most of us to limit the number of boxes we frequent. This used to be called keeping your place.

Thus lunchroom aides and school aides are rarely invited to staff parties although the custodial staff and the Parents Association presidents seem to have made that social breakthrough. Our business with parents tends to be involved with their complaints about us, or much more devastatingly to the point, our complaints about their kids. Certainly we share few social occasions with parents. A rare one at our school was the annual feast in honor of Puerto Rican Discovery Day. Parents cooked ethnic goodies like mad and stuffed us with them. They never sat and ate with us. They hovered over their pots and their guests but they did not break bread with us. There is a profound difference between food given and food shared. If we had been Bedouin tribesmen, I would have looked nervously over my shoulder as I departed the feast.

5

ON DISCIPLINE, FIGHTING, AND BECOMING A GROUP

In most schools children are tracked so rigorously that there is relatively little change, from year to year, in the composition of a class. The children learn ways of relating to one another that carry over from year to year. They form judgments or accept teachers' judgments early on and continue to accept them unquestioningly for years. Teacher judgments of who is smart and who dull, who is good or who is a problem linger in spite of changes in the children themselves. It becomes an exercise in neurotic power to select a child in a new class who has been burdened for years with the label of fool or scapegoat or problem and set about deliberately to change the class's view of him. It is a task in manipulation, and it is appalling to see how easily children can be manipulated, how they can be made to succumb to new judgments by the new authority figure.

Thus my daughter was forever referring to a classmate as "very popular" in spite of the girl's diminishing popularity. Even when I confronted her with the facts that almost no one chose the "popular" girl out of genuine liking, if one were to take their comments about her seriously, and that few children played with her outside of school, my daughter was very slow in modifying her opinion. She defended it on the grounds that she had formed the opinion independently, although she was at a loss to cite the evidence on which she had based her judgment. From her scattered remarks, the picture emerged of a teacher in the past who had firmly fixed the label on the "popular" girl. Ever since, everybody just knew she was popular, and everyone, to some extent, had concluded that there was something wrong about oneself in not being able to recognize and value and emulate the popular girl's behavior.

It is all part of the way in which words come to dominate reality in school as elsewhere.

Children in tracked classes have difficulty, when, for some reason, they are moved to another class, in finding their place in the new group. The little movement that takes place is mostly the result of geography: moving to a new neighborhood. Within the school, in a tracked system, there is more movement downward than upward. Teachers and supervisors will work harder to get a misfit into a lower track than they will into a higher one, because children who "can't keep up" are more of a problem then kids who find everything easy. One year in Queens I fought to get a bright black boy moved from the average class to the intellectually gifted one. I lost. He was moved one layer up on the grade. "We never jump children more than one step up," my supervisor told me. So his next year's teacher complained, only half jokingly, that he was an irritating child. He never seemed to be doing anything. He was always a monitor. But she could never catch him out. He always had his work done neatly and correctly and, most annoying of all, effortlessly.

Even getting a child out of the so-called Opportunity Class, a catch-all of slow children and behavior problems and educationally retarded children with language or perception or speech problems, is a battle. It took two years, in the same school, to convince people that a little boy with a speech defect should not be sent on to junior high in the bottom group. He had, after all, always been kept in the Op Class.

The rigid tracking serves to freeze social relationships within the class and within the school to an astonishing degree. Besides bringing their own and their teachers' prejudices with them from class to class, from year to year, the children bring their group prejudices with them too. In the school in Queens, the Op Class, predictably, had the most defeated self-images. Some of the gifted classes, flattered by their teachers, developed an elitist snobbery that even carried over into gym, the one class that they were forced to share with their self-acknowledged inferiors. And the tracking continued with increasing impermeability into high school. One of the few benefits of New York's long fall strike of 1968 was that high school kids who helped open their schools found themselves in untracked groups for the first time in their school lives. The discoveries they made about one another as people were beautiful and to some of them shockingly at odds with all they had ever learned about one another before.

In our school in East Harlem, on the other hand, children were not tracked. Going to the other extreme, classes were sorted and re-sorted each year.

Supposedly each class was evenly sorted out: so many good readers, so many problems. But it never worked out so neatly. There were always children who "had to be separated"; there was always one teacher who could "handle difficult children" or who was "good at drawing out the shy ones." Almost half the children in my class the year I kept the log had been held over at one time or another, with little evidence of their having benefited by the experience. (Another year at the same school I had only two children who were "preprimers"—nonreaders, that is—while a neighbor had seven who had advanced that far.)

In any event, there was little carry-over from one year to the next. Children who had learned to function more or less as a group the year before with a wide variety of teachers, from strict disciplinarian to permissive, now found themselves in a new mixed bag, with whatever expectations and routines they had brought with them not only likely to conflict with the new teacher's way of working but with one another's.

Standard advice given by our supervisors was, "Bear down hard in the beginning. Don't let them get away with anything. Then gradually you can let up a little bit."

Such a method is obviously a failure, else why have to begin each year with it? Or, as some teachers discover, have to continue that way all year long? That it fails as a method is most clearly shown in the last months of the school year when panic seizes the supervisors and faculty notes are full of exhortations to hold fast and bear down and tighten up and (in desperation, no doubt) "give meaningful work" or "plan interesting activities."

Whatever the validity of the initial advice, I always found it difficult to follow. I would start out with good intentions about establishing routines and instilling standards. But there were always needed routines I had neglected, from distributing paper to cleaning up after painting to hanging up clothing (especially since my great routine-establishing fervors always took place in September, when children did not wear coats to school and our paint supplies had not yet arrived). And I was always getting caught up in the enthusiasm of the moment, so that I would forget to stop everything to remind people not to call out or not to leave their seats without permission. Also such routines as were important in a freer classroom, for taking care of special materials, planning and sharing activities or in pursuing them independently, I was not aware of, travelling as I was in unfamiliar territory. And I had lamentable blind spots. It did not occur to me that beans and Cuisinaire Rods could be thrown as well as counted.

As a consequence the first month or two were times of turmoil and seeming disorganization. What little I learned about organization and group needs in such a classroom was often the result of trial and error or of discovery of children's hitherto unsuspected needs and behavior.

And each year, to my annual astonishment, I discovered that gradually the chaos was disappearing, the turmoil settling into tranquility. The noise was becoming purposeful. More and more was happening in the class, with less and less time wasted. I would discover that the children were likable as a group and *in* a group.

In a classroom where children have the freedom to talk, to move around, to work in pairs or in small unsupervised groups, one of the first victims is hostility. In September the children arrive full of suspicions, smoldering, their tempers at the ready. Small fights break out. An accidental shove is seen as a challenge to a duel. A glance is an insult to three generations of forefathers (and mothers). It is, I suppose, the street way of finding out about your fellows and it is to a large degree an efficient and effective way. Of course it is not the school way. In school, feelings must be repressed, anger enclosed in a thin and fragile box of good manners and the ritual language of good sportsmanship and forgiveness and brotherhood.

The school does not permit the free expression of emotions. By its constant insistence on order and discipline, the school to a large extent denies the children the opportunity to express their feelings, to experiment and to learn about appropriate and inappropriate ways of relating to other people. So in a very real sense, the only real emotions the school "permits" are those that it cannot control: violent disruptive outbreaks and fighting. The very forms and rituals that the schools impose upon the children guarantee that they will not learn to cope with their feelings in less hostile ways. The schools insure that the children will, instead, increasingly resort to explosion or withdrawal as the only ways open to them for handling unbearable tensions.

Nevertheless, when fighting occurs, I, as the responsible adult, must intervene. Fights are not difficult to cope with, although at the time wearing. In our class we established one basic rule: When two children have so far lost control of themselves as to willingly inflict pain upon one another, we the spectators should feel quiet compassion for them. Under no circumstances may we, by leaping about and screaming and laughing, aggravate their combat and add to the confusion.

The fight having thus been localized to some degree I can then separate the combatants. They are usually quite willing to be torn apart. The very fact that they have chosen the school as the place to fight indicates to me, however inaccurately, that they welcome my intervention. If they really want to fight without interference, I tell them, they should plan to fight after three at a distance far enough from the school so that they will be able to fight in peace to the end.

Sometimes when a meek and fearful child suddenly takes to fighting late in the year, I let him fight a little while, long enough, I hope, to let him take the measure of his own manliness, before I break it up. If such a fight takes place outside my territory (in the playground at lunchtime) and the enraged child comes up to class to get his books and return to whatever punishment outraged authority has decreed, I may even express sympathy and admiration, if I feel it.

Some children take much longer to get over the need to fight. The vigor of their attacks and the undiminished fury that far outlasts the few minutes of physical combat continue to present problems throughout the year. But such a child is rare. Usually, eventually, you learn how to cope with him and he learns to cope with his own anger. Kidding is better than authority, tickling better than physical restraint, a swat better than a lecture. After the breakup, there must be privacy and the time to sulk and salve hurt pride.

It should be said also that physical handling, fondling, minor horseplay, touching—the laying on of hands—was, between fights or on the verge of fights, a gentling experience. It seems to satisfy the need for physical communication that fighting also seems to satisfy. The laying on of hands, the willingness to touch one another, is not somehow encouraged in our society. And for many children the first message of the hands is a hostile one: they seem to expect hands only to hurt them. The lightest touch triggers off a cringing withdrawal and a harsh comment. "Git offa me!" How often one hears the phrase, not only in response to a touch but even to a remark perceived as critical or intrusive.

In my first years of teaching I had to overcome the feelings of restraint and intrusion that accompanied my few impulses to touch a child. It was literally years before I got up the courage to touch a black child's hair, years during which they often touched mine with great interest. I discovered, belatedly, not only what their hair felt like but what a pleasant soft tactile experience it was to pat the gently resistant mass.

In the process I learned to be more tolerant of little girls' continuing interest in combing one another's hair, particularly when I began to recognize it as a way of satisfying a profound curiosity about one another. The little Puerto Rican girls with long smooth hair were often willing participants in the rituals of combing and braiding and tying. In return they would cooperate in the styling of their friends' hair, helping with the rubber bands and bows and clips that still, after years of Afro styling, continue to be such a constricting fashion for so many of them.

Because I had resented the punishment of the comb as a child and had in turn seen my own children's resistance to it, I wonder at the slowness with which the Afro-natural style is taking hold. One can only admire the endurance of the children and feel sad and angry at the prejudices of the culture that make all those wasted hours of hair torture a social necessity.

There is another aspect of prejudice in the laying on of the hands. Having been exposed to and indoctrinated in the business of whites' prejudice against blacks, I was still not prepared for the openness of rejection by little children among themselves. Fair-skinned children would refuse to hold a black child's hand in line, with all the cuteness and impatience with which older children would refuse to hold hands with the opposite sex. And I was not prepared for the reverse. I came reluctantly to recognize that some black children drew back from my touch not in fear but out of a genuine revulsion at my whiteness, and of course some children would make open accusations of bias. When I was sure of my grounds, I would mention the fact, sometimes in hostility, sometimes mildly. It was, even in the short run, healthy to bring out the problem into the open. There was no sense in lecturing about brotherhood or protesting in my own defense. At the most I would ask the child who felt I was picking on her out of prejudice to try to examine the event objectively. Why had I selected her out of a roomful to be the victim of my racism? What was she doing at the time? Or I would tell her and the class that if she really believed I was a racist, then she had the right and the obligation to tell her parents and bring them to school to complain to the principal. The children found this reassuring, but even as I said this, I recognized how futile such a course would be. In licensing teachers, the absence of bigotry in whatever form is not considered as a qualification, perhaps because it is so hard to measure. And no principal I've known would acknowledge the justice of the accusation even if, in a rare case, he might agree with it. For agreement would mean that he would have to assume responsibility and take action. At best he might at term's end encourage the culpable teacher to transfer "voluntarily." At worst he would warn the staff to beware of trouble-making militant parents whose children should be handled circumspectly.

As for myself, beyond the open recognition of the existence of prejudice in the classroom (and the ways in which we responded emotionally to it), I continued to touch a child whenever I felt like it. Sooner or later the wince and the automatic withdrawal would disappear.

After the surface hostility, the open fighting also soon disappeared in my moderately free classroom. Verbal combat continued longer. Sometimes this was replaced early on by the great ghetto pastime of sounding, where children would trade flip and fluent insults by the hour. If the verbal fighting was genuine, not ritual, it could be stopped by a joke or by an invitation to take center stage so that we could all listen to it. On the other hand, sounding became part of our repertory of language games, with children on special occasions forming their own teams and sounding for the tape recorder. They were acid critics of one another's performances. They were willing to discuss what forms of humor were deemed appropriate by the school and to eliminate toilet and sex jokes. Some even discovered upon examination that many of the taboo insults were not really very clever at all, relying as they did on the taboo for the predictable effects of shock and laughter. Girls liked to participate, but they often had had little practice in the art form. It was a rare, and much admired, girl who could handle the ritual with skill.

Sounding also became a source of information about the children. Who were the most adept, sensitive to the uses of language, able to switch from one vein to another with skill and wit? Which children tended to get bogged down in a litany-like pattern, working variations on one theme until it was threadbare and they were reduced to repeating themselves, unable to shift to a new line of attack? And they revealed their secret information. as they dipped into their reading and television viewing for apt and crushing similes. A hitherto silent child who indulged in a stream of "Yo mothuh a dinosaur, yo mothuh a tyrannasaurus rex" gained the admiration of the class while he clued me into his secret passions. And some of the children who were not very good at it would go home and practice sounds and write them out and bring them in to read laboriously, word for word, while their classmates listened with great interest and sympathy.

In the first month or two in a classroom the children and the teacher go through a period of mutual exploration and of growing trust. The sooner the children get to know one another the better. Given the opportunity to choose activities, they have also the chance to choose working partners. My observation of these partnerships was quite casual, concerned as I was with what the children were doing rather than with whom they were doing it.

In the increased exposure of a freer classroom, the individual child has to be seen as an individual person, not as a member of a smaller or larger group role-playing at being a student. His choice of friends inside the school is not limited to his tastes as a social being, but reflects his deep feelings about himself as a capable, worthy person. In the classroom this view must include his role as a student, and to a degree exclude his other selves: part-time worker in neighborhood stores, playground champion, mother's reliable assistant.

Until the middle of the year of the log, I was unaware of the extent to which children seek one another out in the classroom for support, for camouflage, for protection against the harsh judgments of the school, for defense against the common enemy.

Seating arrangements in the beginning were quite arbitrary. To the extent that they had the choices available, children who were functioning at a very low level and who lacked self-confidence seemed to choose partners in two directions. Some would seek out the best and quietest (most passive) students, not for help in learning but as a source to copy from and a prompter in emergencies. Others, finding comparisons invidious and having no great desire simply to turn in work, anybody's work, would seek out playing partners, other children with whom they could goof off and fool around, allies against the teacher, kids who, being equally bad and incompetent, did not threaten their fragile souls.

In our desert classroom, full of textbooks and little else, almost all the children tended to select games that were too easy for them or books that were too easy. Even the best readers would take primers and read them to one another or latch onto the simplest phonics games or picture lotto. Sometimes they would find a child or be sought out by one who was really incompetent. He then became their audience, admiring their skill and participating timidly and for short stretches of time.

Better students would often seek partners who could do the same kind of work so that they could indulge in a competition of productivity. But even this was at a low level of interest and challenge. The output and the comparing interested them more than the task itself, or else they enjoyed the social amenities involved, much as though they were at a quilting bee.

And while the members of the class were discovering one another in small safe tasks, they were also tending to fragment, to find safe groupings from which they did not venture. I felt that the fragmentation served also to protect them from "strangers," satisfying a need to withdraw from more demanding relationships that they were not sure they could handle.

To overcome the fragmentation, it became necessary to involve the children with one another as a group. I rearranged the desks into a horseshoe for a while. The children were then always exposed to one another. I used to be shocked to discover late in the school year that my own children did not always know the names of every child in their class. What deprivation it is to be nameless! In the informal classroom children learned to know one another better, but still there were some isolates or members of alien groups who were ignored. Children tended to be quite exclusive and indifferent to the outsiders. We needed to know one another not only as individuals or as members of our particular subsets of the group but as a class. We needed to belong to one another.

And we needed also to talk to one another in the large group. Too often the classroom becomes a puppet, the strings all in the teacher's hands. She pulls a string, a part moves in response, but its movement and direction are unilateral. The other children feel no need to participate, not even by listening. The mere physical fact of confrontation forces an awareness of one another. The strings get all tangled up.

The encyclopedia became a marvelous instrument for opening up groups. The initial exposure to the set of books was in terms of what John Holt calls "messing around." The books had sat on the shelf neglected by almost all the children. So I simply distributed the volumes at random and sat back. They leafed through, fascinated by the abundance and variety of the pictures, and gradually, by the topics themselves. Some children found naked statues or the overlays of the frog, transparent page after page of the frog's innards. Others found animals and flags. Some began to wonder if a favourite topic might be found, and they had a flurried excited game to see if the topic they thought of was in one of the books. It took only a few moments to explain how they could locate a subject or relocate it.

After that introduction they returned to the books again and again. Mostly they looked at the pictures, clustering together to have profound conversations about the poisonous possibilities of various animals, or murmuring in awe that people's kidneys looked like the kidney beans they had been planting. Sometimes the encyclopedia coalition would be quite surprising, drawing together such diverse emotional and educational types as Ann, the masochist, compulsive Seth, aggressive Walter a reader at first-grade level, Carl the hyperactive, Diana the charming butterfly and Richard the dilettante, drifting in and out. That such an abrasive and erratic crew could function together so peacefully was a shock to me.

As the children in the class became more aware of one another and got to know one another's skills and interests, so many of their subgroupings became more flexible. Thus the arts and crafts crew could include in their tight little company other children whose skills they needed or whose interests temporarily coincided with theirs.

But for children to share openly in the large group, trusting the large group to accept them, was not so easy. For children who have failed so often it is a risk to expose themselves again. The most successful children can accept others' mistakes with calm indifference. But the bottom of the heap—how they mock one another, call out insults, shout with laughter, flay one another, till the group is raw and quivering. I had to protect them from their own self-protective cruelty. With a harshness I usually avoided I put them down, condemning them for their intolerance, insisting on their right to make mistakes without the class's brutal intervention. If some child, impatient with the burden of some small bit of knowledge, called out an answer in contempt while another was still struggling, I accused him of showing off. "You are saying to him, 'You're dumb. I'm smarter than you.'" When a child persisted in the mockery, then I would, with the cruelty all teachers possess, show him up, selecting a passage too difficult, a question he could not answer. Then I would defend him from the mockery of his classmates.

They were relieved by my unexpected show of power. It was not, after all, a game they enjoyed playing. Soon they gave it up. After a while they even began to relax, to give one another small praise, eventually learning to correct another child in a mild and helpful way. They would even turn upon a new member of the group who still did not know that he did not have to play the game. "Whatcha doin that for? He got feelins, ya know? Wait till you make a mistake, you like people laughin at you?"

The wearing-down process, smoothing out the rough and abrasive edges until the children all seemed to fit together, went on almost invisibly, month after month.

The children gave evidence along the way that they were learning to accept one another and, more importantly, themselves. Substitute teachers discovered that they were an easy class to cover in my absence. In the fall they had not been so kind to subs.

Interestingly, the significance of another small event escaped me for a long time.

The first school day of the new calendar year, the desks were all jumbled together at one side of the room, untidy evidence that over the holidays the classrooms had undergone one of their two annual floor washings and waxings. I told the children that they could arrange the desks to suit themselves.

The good students chose good students to sit near; the failure-prone chose failure-prone. This almost completely reversed the early fall pattern where the failure-prone had tried to sit next to the "smart" kids. The children had made the transition from dependency to independence, to seeking out genuine working partners. They sought out kids who were working at or near their own levels in reading and math, with whom they could team up for tasks. Obviously they were relying more on themselves and their own efforts. Certainly they had learned to trust themselves enough so that they were no longer so threatened by the negative feelings which ability-labeling had always given them.

The most difficult kids, George and Walter, Carl and Julio, had also teamed up, forsaking their chosen or enforced isolation. (To my horror, though, they sorted themselves into acting-out partnerships, each pair including one strong and one weak member.) Another kid difficult to reach, Richard, who had made a pretense of sitting within the general group, withdrew completely from the class arrangement of desks, finding himself a floating single desk well outside the group. Belinda and Karen, both bashful and withdrawn in class (although in the yard they were as lively as kittens), formed a partnership. Both had always sat with the most successful girls they could find. John, accepting his own cleverness at last, no longer needing to hide it, sat with Seth.

Thus did the children testify that they had come to terms with themselves and with me. It seemed we had learned to trust one another with the most vulnerable and private information that we had about ourselves in school. We were at last free to risk disclosing our weaknesses and our strengths and to get down to the business of learning.

It is hard to point to a time and say, now we are working as a group. But special days, like the day after New Year's, brought the process into focus.

At the Christmas party, before the holidays, the children had still been abrasively separate. As they made the rounds, distributing the goodies they had brought in, many still acted like suspicious and hostile strangers, grabbing up candies, snatching another person's share when he wasn't looking, breaking into small exclusive social groups, being noisy and rough. Only Walter seemed to gain from the experience. Until then he had had only a negative impact on the group, because he was argumentative, disruptive, nonfunctioning. Now, gorging himself fantastically, he wound up the afternoon the center of admiration and attention as he displayed a distended belly as curved and hard as a watermelon.

The change that had come over them was visible at the Easter party, where they were as dainty and peaceful as any group of well-bred friendly adults. They TALKED to one another, they shared their food, they didn't gorge or throw popcorn around the room. They had had no lessons in etiquette in the interim, no opportunities to practice the party ritual. They had simply grown up a little bit. They had learned to accept and even like one another.

We adults make growing up much harder than it needs to be. Children, having little objectivity and less experience, are often possessed of strange and ludicrous and sometimes terrifying misconceptions about the world and themselves. This data they usually keep secret from adults and from most of their peers, because they assume that no one will be very interested and besides they are convinced that what they have come to know and believe is such common knowledge that it does not bear talking about. Or they are afraid they will be laughed at.

When we impose upon children our school values of silence and passivity, our public judgments, our emphasis on reliance on experts, we imprison the child within himself. In the freer classroom, relaxed, engrossed, full of interaction and transaction, full of a diversity of humanity—good or bad, strong or weak, clever or dull—one of the subjects the child learns a lot about is the difficult art of being a person among people.

TEACHERS AS STUDENTS

A teacher is enraged because we did not collect the papers after making an assignment. How alike teachers and kids are. They pay no attention to the learning involved in doing the paper and in the general discussion that follows. All that signifies is that there will be no mark, no recognition for a task completed.

Assignments are assignments. You don't do one if you can get away with it. And if you misjudged and did it, then there are the ritual expectations to be met. Talk of motivation! We see the kids as not motivated to learn, but here are teachers who have joined a workshop out of a strong need for mutual help. And they react like kids.

They no more think than the kids do, no more question the assumptions that they work and fail by than do the kids. They no more dream of making change or demanding change or *wanting* change than the kids do. They set their classes up in groups because it's expected. Unless they wind up with twenty separate groups, the chances are that each of the three or four groups considered an efficient workable number will contain within it a three or four years' spread in functioning levels. But they don't look at what is happening. They do not even consider whether learning can take place in any other terms but those of their own school experience: written work, drill, ability groups, neatness, fulfilment of assignments, size places, following instructions, wrong and right answers.

We are like priests of an ancient religion. The visions have deserted us but the rituals remain. We feel threatened by the heretics who question the rituals. God forbid we should go back and question the visions themselves!

So we recite our catechisms: question and answer; and heaven is assured. That there should also be the damned is only to be expected.

JULIO

He brought me his plant tray. He had stuck a twig in it bearing a huge sign: "Julio plant is dead." It was the one dead plant out of the dozen or more bean plants flourishing.

Months later Julio wrote a story. He always wrote about food and I told him for once to write about something else. He wrote a few lines, dopey inept jokes about shoes "and then I put dirt in and a seed and the plant died." I can see him now. Freddy has mentioned frogs in some far-fetched connection to baskets—another idiot—and Julio minutes later is making his Adam's apple dance, and his bowtie, bulging his eyes and making frog sounds. Writing his story he sits at a loss, rolling his eyes and simpering. He sees our plants and, born loser, proceeds to plant a seed in his shoe and it dies. Pathetic fat greedy little twelve-year-old trying to be funny and a little bit daring, to impress his peers, not daring enough to include girls in his story but thinking how lewd and devilishly clever he is. And he cannot bear it and he kills his plant. All things die for Julio. Poor Julio.

ART

The children think they like to draw but when they are given the chance to do so the experience is often unpleasant. Little girls and boys will reach for the black crayon, draw a series of intersecting curves and then proceed methodically and patiently to fill in each space with a different color. Damn the first-grade teacher who taught them that.

Or there is always one Diana who can draw girls. She has built a reputation on her ability to turn out identical Betty Boops by the dozen. The others come to her and ask her to draw her figure on their paper. Or sometimes it will be a boy who has mastered Batman or a dog or lion or Charlie Brown. And there are always two or three who claim they want to draw, begin some wretched design based on dreams of glory and end up in a rage scratching black crayon or paint all over it and crumpling up sheet after sheet. Gradually they veer off into fooling around and throwing crayons around the room and getting into fights. If I am lucky, I catch them before the point of no return and set them to housekeeping tasks to distract them.

I found some how-to booklets in an art supply store and brought them to class. The children loved them because the formal step-by-step instructions helped them to achieve results that pleased them. After all they do have criteria and do apply them to their own work with a critical harshness that would devastate most adults.

The few formal lessons that we had dealt with rough figure

On Discipline, Fighting, and Becoming a Group

sketching, with children posing for one another. Or we "really looked at" a window or a tree and tried to draw them.

Even when they looked at a tree, their pictures still came out the same way: a fat trunk, closed at the top, with the branches stuck on like crooked tines of a fork. I finally figured out what was happening, to our mutual delight. The trunk enclosed space, the branches did not. By the simple expedient of making each of the single-line branches thicker, doubling the lines, spacing them more widely where they joined the trunk and tapering off at the tip, we got quite handsome, realistic trees.

So they really were seeing how the branches grew out of the trunk. They just hadn't figured how to represent them except at the most abstract diagnostic level.

6

BATTLEGROUND AND STALEMATE

Teachers are always looking for answers to the question of why children fail. At any level, our search for new techniques or for gimmicks is a genuine response to a genuine need to succeed at our task.

But each answer in turn is discovered to be only a piece of the truth. For example: observing the ways in which a nonstandard dialect, with its different rules of pronunciation and grammar, interferes with the process of learning to read, I attacked the reading problem from that point of view. The linguistic approach worked well. Children could see structure and could sound out the words. But now I was confronted with the children's problems in comprehending what they could "read." I observed the complexities of syntax, the way in which children seemed often to be insensitive to or unaware of the syntactic clues to meaning. So we worked at meaning within the sentence. The lessons were delightful and fruitful for most of us. But again, at the end of the year, there was the terrifying fact that a certain number of children had not benefited at all. Was I prepared to write them off as ineducable? Were there really children who could not learn? Or whom I could not teach?

By all the rules of logic and careful pedagogy, the children should have learned. But the rules did not apply. I began more and more to feel that it was useless to look for new answers. What was needed was new questions. Not *why do children fail?*—not again. But *why do teachers—why do I fail?* What is going on that I do not see, or do not want to see?

One question I was not prepared to ask: why was I willing to continue to work in the public schools and to support, by my participation, a hostile and unyielding system?

As long as I could play games of classroom management and "innovation" I could avoid facing up to my disturbing doubts about the whole educational process and my role in it. I could continue to indulge in compromises which were and are betrayals and surrenders, as long as I could continue to view myself as the gallant fighter at the barricades, battling against insuperable odds for miniscule gains.

Time and again, when I could not permit myself to quit and walk away and when I could not hide from myself that I was failing to achieve my goals, I searched for reasons for the failure. In the process, the focus would shift, so that now I was not fighting on behalf of the victims against the powerful enemy. The victims would become, in subtle and brutalizing ways, a part of the enemy force which I had to overcome.

In bad times, the images are all hostile. Sleep is drenched in nightmares: guerilla warfare, ambush in the jungles, nuclear chain reactions, the keeper in Bedlam locked in with the grinning psychotics by inadvertant and indifferent authority; and individually: death death death. I wish you would die, I want you to die.

In some classes the children resist with unabated energy month after month, and teacher and child go on fighting, battling like dinosaurs unconscious of evolution but heading blindly toward extinction. There is nothing at all in such a classroom but fatigue— enormous, oppressive fatigue. Such a classroom is the scene of a power struggle which can only be won by sadists or psychopaths.

The class the year I kept the log was not like that. Many of the children accepted my relatively unorthodox ways with goodwill and enthusiasm. Many more were so cowed that they had no will to resist me or any authority figure.

But there were some who were so trapped by their own rigid responses to their own internal reality that they could not modulate their behavior to deal with a reality outside themselves.

More and more I had to try to understand the children, to see how, or if, I could cope with them, if not to meet their needs at least to satisfy mine.

George never ceased to be a big problem to me. He sat alone. He did nothing, attempted nothing. He could not read. Good-natured, neatly dressed, smiling, he seldom shared in any of our activities. He was an agitator, setting the other children into turbulent motion and then sitting back, smiling, the detached observer. He insisted on a "one-to-one relationship." Translated the jargon meant that if you did not give him your total attention for a lesson he would not, by himself, in a group, do anything at all. He refused to work with anyone but the teacher and such work as he did then was only for as long as the teacher sat by him guiding him step by step. What elegant blackmail, and how impossible to pay off!

I turned to the guidance counselor for help, and arranged a meeting with her. She advised: Pay more attention to him. She let me read his case history: "Needs one-one relation, intensive remediation, phonics. . . ." Really. The file also disclosed that he had a perception problem, specifics undisclosed. He was supposed to be attending a special clinic but the state had cut off the funds needed. He had special equipment and prescribed exercises which he was supposed to follow at home but did not. I suggested that he come to the guidance counselor for a few minutes periodically to pursue his exercises under her eye. Oh no, you can't do that! Then how about dropping in to visit with him occasionally in class? Just a friendly moment or two at unexpected times. The standard response: Guidance counselors cannot work with children in the classroom. They must not be associated with a punitive atmosphere.

Battleground and Stalemate

After that there was little to be said worth saying. The visit deteriorated into idle gossip about some other children in the class. Talking about Delores, a voluptuous, ugly child who was often absent, the counselor looked embarrassed. "Her parents are institutionalized for antisocial behavior," she said. There was a long silence while I tried to translate that into basic English. "You mean they are in jail?" "Oh please, I can't bear to use that word in school."

She promised to follow up on George. He continued to be a problem because I refused to accept his terms and was not able to devise terms acceptable to him. I would not indulge him with monitor jobs. (Hell's Angels at the rock festival in California—the ultimate in the bully-boy-for-monitor philosophy.) I would not permit him to go visiting his past teachers at will, at odd times during the day. I would not let him draw or wash the sink by the hour. I kept insisting that he work and he kept insisting that he could not. When I ignored him and he sat idly alone he would quickly grow bored and start throwing things around the room. It was a big year for spitballs, Cuisinaire Rods, beans, airplanes, crayons.

The problem of George was eventually solved for me—not for him. As I kept pestering the counselors for help they eventually found some perception exercises which he could or should do. These were elementary and he worked through the stack in a half hour. Then again weeks of waiting and pestering. At last they concluded that I was not meeting his needs and he was transferred to another class. After that I saw him often, because he was promptly made monitor of the audio-visual equipment. He threaded film projectors and sorted, delivered, and collected equipment. He had memorized all kinds of appropriate labels in order to perform these tasks, but he did not learn to read. He dropped in on his rounds for smiling brief visits with us and in other ways kept himself so usefully busy that he did not have time to learn to read. But at least the constant barrage we had been living under tapered off and gradually disappeared completely.

Julio was another one. He had no confidence at all and so did nothing at all. He was quiet most of the time, although George (while he was in the class) and Carl could often suck him into the whirlpool of their unrest. Unlike them, who had had years of practice at disrupting and knowing when to retreat, he did not know what the unwritten limits were. So he got carried away on a turbulent silly sea, spinning round and round, making stupid jokes, clowning, not knowing when to stop. He was a fat boy, big for his age. What little attention he had ever gotten had been paid for in advance by the humiliation of playing the fool and being the butt.

The year before I had had his sister. She didn't act the fool. But she complained that she did not understand the work. What little she did seemed mostly to have been copied from others. I tried sympathy with her, figuring that if I removed the pressures that seemed to overwhelm her and did not make demands on her that she obviously could not let herself meet, and if I praised her for small returns, she would begin to relax and to progress. But it didn't work. At the end of the year she was as slow and fearful as she had been at the beginning. What little she had learned she did not know that she had learned, so that it was an almost useless increment for her. And she went on to the end copying, cheating, turning in neat papers, complaining that she didn't know what to do.

When I saw Julio enter my class I was depressed. Here was another one, a loser, doomed and damned. And a smiling loser to boot, alternating foolish smiles and vacant stares with a rare case of the sulks. I had no idea how to cope with him. I couldn't stand him.

There he would sit with the simplest assignment, writing his heading over and over and over, crumpling up the sheets, starting all over again and in the end doing nothing at all.

The ritual of the heading was most interesting. Children learn the heading very early in their school careers. On one side their name and class, on the other the date and the school. For children like Julio it becomes a refuge, a way of avoiding the task. For most children it has become a compulsion. In their notebooks, page after page bears the heading, even though the sheets are stitched in and will never be removed, and even though most of the rest of the page will be blank. I tell them that I do not want them to waste their time writing headings. A date will do, and their name if the sheet is to be collected. They are offended by my attitude. I am taking away from them not only a sacred rite but a useful crutch, a technique for postponing the time when they must get down to work. They argue in favor of the heading. Some, like Julio, never give it up.

Diana and Belinda also relied on headings to use up the bulk of their working time. Diana made a great show of interest and enthusiasm, but she did little work and she did not learn. She was flip, a butterfly, seemingly outgoing and friendly. But she was full of hidden malice, a tease, and most of the other children saw through her charm. Only Ann clung to Diana in a tenuous friendship, and Diana made the most of it. One day as we were lining up Ann was in tears because her briefcase had disappeared. We searched high and low, none more assiduously and sympathetically than Diana. When at last it became clear that we would not leave the room until the bag was found, Diana smilingly confessed that she had hidden it, and she brought it to Ann. And Ann, poor Ann, was grateful for the recovery. She left arm in arm with her friend Diana. Diana was manipulative, humiliating Ann at every opportunity, getting her into trouble in and out of school. But that, sadly, was what Ann needed and wanted.

Belinda was quiet, quiet, quiet. She used her bashfulness as a club to fend you off and beat you down. When called upon, her frozen averted gaze outlasted the longest waiting time. Teachers in self-defense learned to baby her, not to push her, to leave her alone. Trapped in a rare confrontation, she resorted to heartbreaking, enduring tears. It was months before she would even speak directly to you and then it would be a secret timid approach, sidling up and whispering so that you had to bend toward her and focus intensely on the mumbled phrases. She even, for a long time, used emissaries to ask permission for her to go to the bathroom.

Ann, the masochist, Diana's friend, was a good reader but a poor student. From other teachers she extracted special sympathetic treatment and extravagant praise, and I observed enviously that she did produce beautiful stories for them. But she could not stand being successful and outstanding. It did not fit her world view. So each good story was followed by weeks of forgetting homework or careless errors or chattering or breaking things until she had paid the terrible debt.

Ann usually stayed within the bounds of expected behavior. But sometimes out of some dreadful need she exposed herself to the worst kinds of punishment. Thus in gym, after all the children had been warned not to chew gum, she, who seldom chewed, had gotten some bubble gum and begun with amateur vigor and incompetence to chew most publicly. The gym teacher decided to punish the whole class for her infraction, threatening them all with missing the next gym class. The children turned upon her.

When I was a child, I lived on a chicken farm. Sometimes a chicken would bleed from a chance wound. When the other chickens, nervy and skittery, saw the blood, they moved in to attack. Cannibal chickens, they would peck and peck until the victim lay dead.

The day Ann chewed gum, the children in the classroom turned upon her, cannibal chickens seeing blood and moving in for the kill. She sat there calmly resigned to this confirmation of her expected and deserved fate, making no gesture in her own defense, seeming almost to be sadly enjoying it.

I cut the children short. Pretending to want the facts, I let them, within limits—no more blood—relieve themselves of their anger at the injustice of the punishment. I offered to intercede with the gym teacher, isolating Ann for punishment. But I was furious with Ann. She was too much like me, or like what I once was, the passive helpless victim, not even cringing from an attack.

Sometimes I tried to talk to her about her participation in the catastrophes that befell her. Yes, yes, she would say, smirking, her pale little face made uglier by the fusty lank hair, the too-large glasses slipping down her nose. But she did not change. After a storm had passed, when everyone, exhausted by their anger and by the strenuous effort to beat against her unresisting mass and by the consequent guilt, abandoned her, then she would curl up into a small fragile ball and weep quietly, persistently, until the children near her could not bear it any longer and turned against me, demanding that I DO something.

I came to look upon her tears—and those of others—as an aggressive act. In Ann's case, I would explain to the children, "If she wants me to know what's the matter, she will tell me." But they would be angry at my seeming indifference. They would circle around her, hugging her, consoling her, putting their dear little heads down till they touched, whispering comfort in her ears. And how she flourished, her tears feeding now from the fountain of their concern.

I wasted no sympathy on tearful children. Take a friend and go to the bathroom and freshen up. Come back when you're calm again. Even boys, reduced by their impotence to tears of rage, would welcome such treatment. In deference to their masculinity I would often explain to their mocking classmates that the tears were not sissy. They were a sign that the child was mad enough (at me, at a classmate) to want to kill. Since that was out of the question, the child had sensibly, but obviously at great cost, decided against attempting it. Thus the tears were the product of outraged manhood trying to gain control of itself. The boys would recognize the feeling and stop their laughter, making small secret gestures to the upset child: Welcome to the club of the put-upon and impotent.

But Ann was different. She sat stubbornly in her chair, refusing to remove herself from our troubled vision. She sucked me into her tragic games with the class or with her grandmother. Wanting to prove something to her about reality as opposed to her narrow bleak vision of the world, I became a participant in her masochistic games in which the victim victimizes the whole class by her very weakness, using the teacher as the instrument of her revenge. How many times did I promise myself that I would not be drawn in again?

Luisa and Linda, quiet and polite, had mastered the techniques of seeming productive while barely learning anything. They were so good, by school definitions, that they reduced themselves to near invisibility. They turned in neat pages of work, they never raised their hands, they seemed always far away and only rarely were they caught out in their ignorance. They seemed so nice and shy that teachers were reluctant to embarrass them by insisting on their participation. But occasionally I would force the issue.

Linda was tuning out as usual one day when I pounced on her for the answer to a simple problem we were working on, converting seconds into minutes. A neighbor fed her the answer. How solicitous her friends were, how concerned because I was picking on her and hurting her. So they fed her the answer and as usual she relayed it to me. I refused the answer and continued the attack. What was the process? How did you get the answer?

Her little friends—you could almost see the waves of protectiveness—they turned away from me, their shoulders formed a series of arcs, a wall to shield her from me. Their heads leaned toward her yearningly. They were too intimidated to offer further help, but their lips moved as though the inaudible internal vocalization might somehow reach and rescue her.

The incident brought into focus the primacy of symbolic behavior, the unreality of the relationships in the classroom, the role playing, the inhumanity.

We were all involved in a play but we knew our roles by heart. All that love pouring out to protect the defenseless victim of authority. I had thought, after all those months together, that we had at least learned to be real with one another, to trust one another. But while they had let down their guards they had not given them up. Why, I could feel them asking, why was I not satisfied to play the game by the rules? Why was I not, in that particular instance, satisfied with the answer? Why did I have to insist instead on processes and relationships and understanding?

Part of the problem, of course, was that I had not relinquished my *teacher* role. When I was acting like *a teacher*, the children responded to me on those terms. I thought I was becoming more aware of the tense threatening dialogue of classroom life, but I was still, too often, a ready participant in it.

One day, when I was setting up groups, planning to work with—"teach"—the problem children, Migaly said she did not want to work with us, her pride offended by her inclusion. She wanted, she claimed, to listen to stories on the tape recorder. When I refused her, recognizing in her choice another avoidance of a necessary and threatening task, she enticed Linda into a sulky, trivial mood. Furious with me for not yielding to her, she was not about to cooperate in any activity. The inevitable complaints and fault-finding: YOU stopped me from working, because YOU would not let me do what I wanted to do.

Why shouldn't I let her use the tape? Why did I find it necessary to assert my will and thereby force a confrontation which was time-consuming and irritating and disturbing to the rest of the class?

Since at the time I had not consciously added tape recorders to my list of partial (and therefore unsatisfactory) answers to the problem of education, it all came down to a power play. I had decided what was good for her, and I wanted her to obey. Because she did not accept my authority gracefully, she played upon my own doubts and weakness. I questioned my own authority. I distrusted myself as the competent adult in a roomful of children. I had to act out my authority in self-defense.

Of course the teacher will always, sooner or later, win in a confrontation. There is too much on her side. There are too many legitimate ways to get at a child. But in the middle of the struggle I forget where the power really lies. I become involved in the game with the child as though power and position and all such irrelevant abstractions existed in the real world of the classroom to be fought over with a child as though we were *equals*.

Eventually, if imperfectly, I learned how to avoid most confrontations. I learned to permit the child his pathetic little face-saving displays. I learned to trust him and myself. But how much time I lost in the learning, and how distracted I was from the real issue—how to get Migaly to be willing to learn so that she did not need to escape to the false refuge of the earphones or the only partially false delusions of hostile teachers. The confrontation which she daily faced was her failure and her fear of it, and I was nowhere near knowing how to cope with that.

At the time all I learned was what I already knew. School is a jail. Even if I tried to take down the bars, I knew and the children knew that the bars were still there and that all I have done is to plant green hedges between us and them. But I was also oppressed by my own inconsistency. I wondered if I was not playing one more trick on them, conning them with the illusions of freedom of choice and decision making, of responsibility for their own actions, while ultimately and arbitrarily and recognizably I was not one of them: I was one of the wardens.

Beyond me were others who controlled me, who could at will and arbitrarily impose their rules and procedures on us all. It really didn't matter that I was concerned about the failure of the children and that was why, I rationalized, I must intervene, as I had with Migaly. It was small consolation to realize that the school imprisoned me, the teacher, as much as it did the child. Perhaps the realization made matters even worse, because I was always conscious of the barbed wire while the children seemed able to function for long peaceful periods as though the walls did not exist.

The problem of the children who could-not/would-not/did-not learn grew more inescapable as time went on. As the worst disruptive behavior diminished, as some children took off in productive and happy activity, we seemed to be sorting ourselves out into two groups. In a way I resented the ones who most needed my help. It was so much more fun to go skylarking around the world with the eager and adventurous children, opening windows and doors for them, finding new roads to send them chasing down. How impossible it was to find the time and the patience and the materials for those others who would not, without coaxing and pushing and pulling, take even the smallest first steps. When I found an activity they enjoyed, I tended at first to indulge them in it, and only when it became clear to me that the activities they enjoyed were the most passive and undemanding ones, from which they learned little, would I retreat in irritation. As in the case of Migaly, I found myself occasionally puritanically discouraging them, without knowing how to substitute something that they could accept.

Listening to the tape recorder was one of the passive activities that the slowest readers loved. They sat, earphones in place, eyes on the pages of the book, following the stories. Children who were restless and who never listened to me, like Belinda and Julio, soon discovered the safety of the tape recorder and sat for long stretches of time hearing the same stories over and over. They surprised me by their requests. Would I tape *The Gingerbread Man* and *The Three Billy Goats Gruff*? They were fifth graders. Were these really favorite stories? Or were they more likely simply familiar stories which the children knew almost by heart and which they could, after listening to them again and again, read to themselves with comparative ease, finding small pleasure in small success? Or were the stories associated in their short memories with the golden days of kindergarten where nothing was a failure and where no one insisted on their "doing" anything with a story but enjoy it? For every child, like Karen, who benefited from the exposure, there were half a dozen for whom it was simply a socially acceptable form of escape.

I continued for a long time, though, to permit most children their escapes, partly in self-preservation, partly because I did not know what else to substitute, rationalizing that they would, willy-nilly, learn something from their low-level participation. But I would become impatient sometimes when they proved to me that they were learning very little.

If only because I could not abide Julio, I began to stand over him during lessons, doing penance in a way, encouraging him to go one step further, insisting over and over that (a) he could do the work and (b) he must do it. Sometimes he would work only while I was policing him. Sometimes he would continue for a little while on his own. Once, during a spelling lesson, while we were developing a list of words in which *ow* sounds like *o* (throw, snow, blow) he woke from his customary lethargy and started offering all kinds of words with *o* sounds. Naturally most of them did not have the *ow* spelling and had to be included in a side list. But he had heard the sound and for once was taking risks, volunteering like crazy for a change, almost reckless in his participation. Afterwards, satiated and peaceful—or perhaps alarmed at his own boldness—he retired into himself again, copying the lists off the board over and over in his exquisite small handwriting.

Julio came to symbolize for me the kids I couldn't work with. Why were they so infuriating? When I tried, one day, to see the pattern behind my feelings, looking at each troublesome student in turn, it was not surprising that Julio should head the list.

Julio. In his avoidance of failure, he had withdrawn almost completely into inaction. The rare instances when he participated were frustrating in their reckless incompetence, in the ninny-aspect of total abandon. It was as though he were diving off a cliff with his eyes shut in the dark. It was hard for me to see in his behavior any kind of growth and consolidation, no matter how slow.

Carl had withdrawn too. But his mother bugged him at home, so he made small unhappy increments in learning. In another way he was not like Julio. He was not a clown or a fool. Even George, I thought, was preferable in some small degree to Julio. Very small degree. To the extent that George could still show some overtly direct hostile behavior he was, I thought, still real, still in touch with his feelings and, so, still accessible. To that degree I could put up with him better than I could with Julio. (Although I could not seem to teach him anything at all.)

Freddy. He worked more than Julio but he too acted the clown, showing no anger.

Diana, another clown in a way. She simpered and smiled, full of false charm plus a string of disrespectful acts barely disguised by cuteness.

Ann angered me, but in a different way. She was so masochistic, so patently and quixotically in pursuit of failure and humiliation.

It was not, I thought at the time, underachievement, not the pursuit of failure, not apathy alone that got to me—as with Belinda. Not pathetic deceitfulness, like Luisa's, as she covered up her lack of understanding by copying, copying, trying to win approval one way or another. It was not avoidance of work, low standards, false fronts and showing off—Richard.

Year in, year out, the children whom I disliked were the ones like Julio, Freddy, Bertie last year, Ronnie the year before. The kids who were never angry, the tragic infuriating smilers who walled themselves in behind idiot masks, who denied and to a great extent no longer felt the vital black emotions. I could not or would not reach them.

I told myself that they needed an authoritarian atmosphere. They needed a cause-and-effect-and-no-excuses environment. Maybe I was just wishing the problem they presented would disappear. Maybe I thought they did better in other classrooms (on the testimony of past teachers, although certainly not on the evidence of their accomplishments to date) simply in contrast to how badly they did with me. They couldn't obviously do any worse than this.

Karen, an underachiever, patient, trusting, hardworking, demanded very little. She was a textbook case in nonstandard dialect, her soft voice slurring gently the word lists I asked her to read. She taught me by the errors she made and the difficulties she encountered, and she accepted gracefully and quietly the small gifts of love I made her.

Maria—I admired her. She was smart and spunky. In the Spanish world of quiet girls and honored boys, she had emerged with fire and independence. I wasn't sure I liked her.

John had wit and imagination. Physically expressive, an actor. We liked each other. At some nonverbal level we were equals, accepting each other's idiosyncracies with tolerant amusement, sharing delightful secrets about life and mankind and the absurdity of school. He understood and was amused by my obscure jokes. This last is no small gift to a teacher. The humor of children is such that they will roar at jokes of the nine-lashes-with-a-wet-noodle variety. It is diminishing, to say the least, in the midst of a burst of laughter at some unexpected turn of language or events, to look down at the startled uncomprehending faces before me. Children in any event are rarely exposed to humour in their teachers or their texts. Laughter is one of the least heard sounds inside the school.

Walter was a violent little boy, open in many negative ways. We had begun to form an unspoken alliance of sorts, to work out a treaty: You can learn and I can, will, teach you. We'll show momma and poppa yet. (He got whipped for his report card.)

Shelley was too middle class and ladylike for my tastes. An ideal pupil. But she judged me on her scale of ideal teachers, with their rewards for good behavior and good work, their homework every day and tests and reports to be posted on bulletin boards. I may have been fun, but I was a failure in her eyes.

Luisa—because of her father I was beginning to like her. He was so full of dreams and love and concern for his children that I found myself looking to find what qualities he must see in her.

Seth was disadvantaged in a special sense. He had a tough, rigid, plugging, serious mind. He was ambitious and pesky and hardworking. He did not work on a manipulative level at all (That's baby stuff!), but had to bludgeon his way through with words and numbers on paper. He handled the abstractions of ideas and numbers and words not abstractly, he was not quite clever or free enough, but as though the words and numbers were THINGS which he must handle physically, by phrasing and rephrasing, writing, rewriting, going over and over and over until he had reached a point of mastery that satisfied him. Strange competitive child with wretched clothes and egg on his chin. Disadvantaged in the sense that his color, his insistence on working verbally, his compulsive persistence, his strong self-imposed patterns of work and drive for achievement put him, in a ghetto school, close to the top in his grade. (Was there also a need to prove that he was better than his social and ethnic inferiors? He was very conscious of color and ethnic backgrounds, very conversant with all the stereotypes, although he managed to get along well with most kids.) John, years below him in reading skills—as scored by the tests—could fly lightly far beyond him into the world of ideas and imagination. So Seth's view of his relationship and his worth to the world was distorted by his virtues. He might, in a more competitive school world, in a rigidly tracked high school, say, have rude and painful confrontations where, despite all his efforts, he would not and could not be Best.

Having taken inventory, though, I was not much further advanced in my thinking about the children, or how to assist those I seemed not to be able to assist. I had admitted to Like and Dislike. I had discovered that some children were more irritating than others. I had exposed and in a sense made real the fact that I responded to the children not so much in terms of their needs as in terms of my feelings and interpretation of their needs. Luisa did not disturb me as much as Julio. I accepted without guilt that I could not cope with George.

But still . . . I had not even bothered to include some children on the list. Perhaps I did not wish to examine them too closely. The arts and crafts crew. I saw them as happy and learning. But they were not learning to read much better. I did not want to have to face my failure with them. Like-dislike may have been a useful exercise for my psyche. But I was still asking the wrong questions. I was still coming up with answers that only served to postpone, but not to resolve, my problem.

THE CLASSROOM AS RITUAL

It has occurred to me again and again that the classroom is a terrible frightening place, the more so because the terrors are hidden and at the same time so well-recognized as to seem inevitable and commonplace. We, teacher and child, tender and accept facsimiles, symbols, rituals which will by custom serve to placate and protect us.

Thus *The Answer*. If you give me the answer, what else can I want? Again and again by my lessons and attitudes I tried to show them that I already knew the answers, I wasn't interested in the answers but in what was happening to them, how they were thinking and understanding and learning. And failing that, at least they should tell me when I had failed. You are the teacher. Show me. Explain so that I will understand. Make me learn.

But we are, both adult and child, conditioned to a classroom where learning and thinking and feeling are not the goals. The externals, The Answer, the conditioned response, the test, the written work checked while the child is safely not checked—the externals are all that matter. Just as, in the teacher's interminable paper work, accuracy does not matter as long as each empty box is filled in so as to be fed to a voracious machine somewhere far away. Just so each failure and success is recorded somewhere on the appropriate blue card and yellow card and white card.

The children have come to me with all their feeble entrenched defenses as I have come to them with mine. And we meet in a sort of demilitarized zone halfway between their real world as real people and my real world as a real person.

Just as they do, so do I go along being a good girl in supervisors' terms for weeks, fulfilling the rituals and following the formulae, hoping only to be left alone and maybe to gain some token of acceptance, some sign of diminished distrust, accepting the compromises which are really distortions and defeats, playing the game, not rocking the boat. And then suddenly the mists clear and I cannot bear to look at where I have been. I cannot bear to look at where I want to go. I pretend that I have not sold out, betrayed myself and worse yet betrayed my children. And there I go in a Rap Brown mood again, wanting to blow up my world because and before it destroys me, even if in the process I am destroyed anyway.

Meanwhile we continue to meet, the children and I, in daily unwilling battle. Slowly, slowly I reach through the cage of my fears and yours and touch you. Child, tell me, who is the prisoner?

SCIENCE

A mother visited class during a science lesson. The children were making a lens by rolling a piece of clear plastic around two pencils, to create a platform, and looking through a drop of water at a scrap of print beneath. When I returned to the classroom after my prep, the mother had completely forgotten about her child or the class. She had made herself a lens and was busy making her own observations.

Seth, all excited: "You can use your own water!"

LANGUAGE

We were talking about regional variations in speech. The children already possess all the negative judgments about "improper" language. His father, Richard announced, came from the South and "it took him seven years to learn to speak correctly."

HOLDOVERS

No matter how often I tell the kids what the policy on holdovers is, many of them do not believe me. They ask again and again, and I reassure them again and again. They cannot evaluate themselves objectively. We talk about next year. For once I would like to have the same class again. Usually, Frank Lloyd Wright's advice is pertinent: Build your failures out in the country, where no one will see them. In the same way, teachers welcome the departure of their failures. Walter, I discover with a pang, still sees himself as a child whom no teacher would want for a second year.

BUSYWORK

I gave the class a math assignment which I clearly identified as busywork, to give me extra time for end-of-term records, a deadline I had to meet.

The kids kept coming up and insisting on help or checks or explanations. My first reaction was annoyance. My second reaction was pleasure. Last October they would have treated the task with apathy, cheating, avoidance—especially since I had so clearly given them an out. But now some at any rate have begun to view my role in a different way, as service and resource. They insisted on my doing my job.

7

AVOIDANCE OF FAILURE

The inventory served at least one purpose. It pointed out that, as far as I could see, my personal antipathies did not closely correlate with the children's success or failure. That is, not all the children I liked were learning. Not all those I disliked were failing. Besides, children would shift, from time to time, from one column to the other. It is easier to dislike children at the beginning of the year than at the end. We learn to live with one another, and the proximity somehow encourages tolerance and acceptance. Only in a rare instance can I maintain a consistently hostile feeling, and when I do, it is usually accompanied by (or caused by?) continuing guilt over failure, either in teaching or in behavior. It is hard to dislike a child who learns while he is with you or who responds to you with some small evidence of trust.

In my reading, I tend to latch on to a phrase or a sentence that seems particularly illuminating, or that promises, if pursued, to lead in a new and helpful direction. So I remembered out of all the Coleman Report a comment about the correlation between the student's feeling that he can control his environment and his achievement. It led, at least, to some new questions. In the spring, 1967, *Harvard Educational Review,* a book review of *A Theory of Achievement Motivation,* edited by John W. Atkinson and Norman

T. Feather, attracted my attention. Most of it was beyond my understanding and patience but one idea remained.

$$T_A = T_S - T_{AF}$$

A person's response Tendency in Achievement-Oriented situations (T_A) is the sum of the Tendency to strive for Success (T_S) and the Tendency to Avoid Failure (T_{AF}). T_{AF} always inhibits responses to achievement-oriented situations. Thus T_{AF} always is subtractive in its effect on T_A.

Why I had even read this far is beyond me. It was not my usual taste in literature. But it brought one aspect of my problem into focus for me. The drive for success is a productive motivation. The avoidance of failure has very negative effects on the learning process.

Teachers are inundated with lectures on motivation. They are told that ghetto children are not motivated to learn. They are instructed, in teaching manuals, for example, in the ways to motivate a lesson. These are dreadful, artificial, gimmicky ways that often, in practice, take more time than the lesson itself and tend to obscure the point of the lesson besides.

But in spite of considerable evidence in our own lives and in our classrooms, we somehow assume that there is either motivation-to-succeed or no-motivation. The book review offered another option, the motivation to avoid failure. For me it was a powerful idea. Setting aside any questions about how the attitude to avoid failure may have been nurtured, I began to play around with the idea as a way of understanding my class.

After all the diagnoses of needs are made, and the plans and materials provided, will the most important element in determining whether a child learns still be the degree to which he tends to avoid failure?

Would Julio ever learn if he could not take the first step: risk error, risk failure? And Luisa? And Belinda? Walter seemed grudgingly to begin to take chances. So did Carl occasionally. The arts and crafts boys seemed to have compartmentalized themselves cautiously. Thus they learned much about science and nothing, relatively, about reading and math. The latter two are school-ritual skills. All the goals of school, all the meaningful successes to be gained in school are tied to these two subjects, *and the children know it.* Science, art, social studies—none of these carry the same weight in elementary school. So none of these has the same pejorative identification with "learning" and with success.

In the next school year after I kept the log, when I complimented a boy on how much he had learned about baseball, he having spent every spare moment poring over books and sports magazines and newspapers, he was surprised. He did not associate baseball with learning. He thought I was putting him on.

What about Delores? She seemed to want to learn, but she could never bring herself to the actual required methodical tasks needed. She withdrew from any formal lessons, no matter how small the group, and resisted even the individual lessons I tried to give her, if I set the terms for their content. On the other hand she read to me one day, from a third-grade (Lippincott) reader, the story of Alice in Wonderland. She made many mistakes but she kept moving along. She participated in her reading, listened to what the words said, interacted with them, laughed at the jokes, recalled incidents in her life that were analagous. I enjoyed the session, but I was uneasy because she had chosen the most inefficient and long-drawn out way to learn to read, full of frustrations for her, if not in my class certainly in the classes to follow. (She told me she used to eat plaster off the walls. Was her dullness an offshoot of lead poisoning?)

Maybe when I was successful in class it was initailly due to the ways and extent to which I could free the children, giving them the courage to risk failure and thereby making it possible for them to achieve small successes. They needed that small breakthrough towards independence and self-confidence. Maybe a test could be devised to determine which children were motivated in what relative amounts by success or by failure, and then provide the classroom atmosphere where they might best function.

Conscious of my failures and of the school's test-oriented pressures, my first solution was self-protective. The failure avoiders would need a very small class with more than one teacher and certainly NOT a permissive atmosphere. (That let me out.) Who are the children who are not functioning in class, either quietly or disruptively? Separate them from the kids who have not learned. The groups are not necessarily identical. The children like Karen who had not learned needed, so I thought, special lessons based on their needs—in her case based on the confusions arising from the mismatch between standard and nonstandard English. But the avoiders of failure, I thought, needed something else besides. They needed an authority which would insist that they must do this and that, to assume responsibility initially for their actions and the consequence of their actions until they grew strong enough to bear it themselves. The avoiders of failure could not easily be challenged or excited or stimulated into doing. Freedom, to Julio, meant the freedom to Not-Do.

A galloping case of avoidance of failure had to be swarmed over, surrounded, drowned in specific kinds of attention. Belinda and Julio, even when forced and bullied into getting down to work, never asked for approval of it or for a check on their results. On the other hand, both would on occasion perform meaningless mechanical tasks ad nauseum. (Julio one day spent an hour writing words from a list over and over.) Homework was useless for them, although it peripherally might provide needed practice for their relatives.

I made up a rough chart of the class. Near each name I put the child's reading level as tested. Then I sorted them out in terms of motivation: Achieving Success or Avoiding Failure. While the children who were most retarded educationally clustered at the Avoiding Failure side of the chart, there were scattered among these some who had learned to read and do math with varying degrees of competence. And on the Achieving Success side were children who

Avoidance of Failure

in their test scores were far behind their abilities: Karen, John, Estabania. You could not draw a bell curve for reading levels that would coincide with a bell curve for success/failure motivation, or for that matter with intelligence or "social adjustment."

As a schema for looking at a class it was fascinatingly tidy. It cut across class, race, home conditions, emotional aberrations, sex, size, innate ability. What one was left with was two loose groupings: those children who were not afraid to try and those who were. The former were a joy to teach. They almost taught themselves. The latter could and would drive a teacher crazy until perhaps she conned herself into believing that all they could do was draw or look at filmstrips and gave them up as ineducable. Or, if she were not so far advanced in self-deception, she might devise a routine authoritarian classroom with the bulk of the work reduced to busywork and repetitive mandated tasks. Write the table of weights and measures ten times, write the spelling words ten times each and use each in a sentence, copy this story, report, letter from the board, look up the meanings of all these words and write them down.

Looking over my avoiders of failure, I found that most fell into two distinct patterns of behavior:

The Conforming Child: He or she is compulsively neat, quiet, "good" or relatively easy to control, undemanding, patient. He will tune out, postpone starting work. "The Perfect Heading Syndrome." Never asks questions or seeks help. Never seeks PRAISE. Likes repetitive, safe, dull tasks. No initiative. Given a choice will choose drawing or doing nothing. Has many excuses: *I didn't hear you. I lost it. I don't understand. I don't got no pencil, paper, book. I was out when you did that* (from children with perfect attendance!). Freezes when called on for an answer. Likes to sit near a quiet bright worker. Cheats. Seems shy. Represses outward shows of emotion, whether anger or joy. Often has good penmanship. Sometimes an isolate or a scapegoat. Sometimes a clown. Has trouble following the simplest directions. Often asks in the middle of a task if he may "finish it for homework." But he will either not turn in homework or will get others to do it for him. Has given up completely.

The Nonconforming Child: Hyperactive, easily frustrated, volatile, a slow starter after many false starts. Gives up in rage, crumpling up the paper over and over again until he subsides into sulky refusal to continue. Tunes out. Doesn't bother to cheat often. Seeks approval via monitor jobs and assumes responsibility for such tasks and does them well. Messy desk, littered floor. Throws things around the room. Blames others: *He made me laugh, He tore my paper. My baby sister tore up my homework. I wanted to do it but you didn't give me enough time. You wouldn't let me do it.* Gum, candy, pumpkin and sunflower seeds by the ton. Sits with other children like him rather than the bright and quiet ones. Forms alliances with other acting-out kids. Teases the conforming ones. An agitator (the children's term for a trouble-maker), setting up fights for others and egging them on. Carries messages of insults, even making them up, to stir up trouble. Writes notes and signs others' names to them: "I love you . . . " or messages containing the powerful "pussy." Occasionally participates in class discussions on nonacademic subjects. Occasionally interested in movies and filmstrips or stories read aloud. Most likely never does homework. Rarely volunteers answers even when he knows them, certainly never responds when called on. Harsh, mocking, jeering critic of others' mistakes. Self-conscious about his failures. Rejects "baby books" in reading or math. Likes to carry visibly "hard" books around with him. If he can, masters some art form (cartoon hero, stylish lady, submarine) and draws it over and over, generously making copies for all who ask. Is still fighting.

Ask a teacher about the conforming child and she will say that he is good, he tries so hard, lovely, so neat, so shy, well-behaved, trustworthy, respectful, interested; alas, he is so dull. As for the nonconformist, send for his parents, though that won't do much good. He is responsible in monitor jobs, but he is so lazy, a chatterbox. Terrible home conditions. I can't turn my back on him.

Avoidance of Failure

He has no self-control, he's not motivated, not interested in learning. He seems bright enough but alas, he is dull.

Ask a guidance counselor for help with a child who avoids failure and she will tell you: he needs a one-to-one relationship. He needs to feel successful. Give him a lot of praise. Let him feel successful at other tasks, monitor jobs, painting. He needs guidance. His parents are really very concerned or else they reject him. And after a time: His needs are not being met in your class. Sometimes a change of class is salutary.

The usual advice to teachers faced with such children is to try and give the children the experience of success in other areas, in drawing, music, monitoring. But that doesn't really work, although it may keep them in beatific quiet while the rest of the class goes about the business of learning. Children do not transfer the feeling of accomplishment from the nonlearning-oriented tasks to the learning-tasks. Indeed, praising them for peripheral and irrelevant activities seems only to reinforce them in their conviction that they are incompetent and inadequate. It's like praising a crippled person for how well he sits up in a wheel chair. There is nothing in that success that will give him the will or the ability to walk—unless he has had to struggle his way to triumph in order to sit up. Then it is not the praise but the experience of mastery that will serve him. To praise a child extravagantly for what any old child seems able, with minimal effort, to do to a teacher's satisfaction can only confirm for him that the teacher shares his belief that he can't do anything at all.

I decided that my first solution to the problem—authoritarianism—was not and had never been the solution. While some learning might take place in an atmosphere of drill and repetition and silence, it would be the most useless fragmented kind. It would be as meaningless and useless and disrupting as the doggerel commercial messages that television "teaches" us. Authoritarianism always has served to mask the problem. The children themselves would not have learned the one thing that mattered to them or that could change their lives. They would not have learned that they could, by their own efforts, take any meaningful action in their own interest. Instead they would have learned the most damaging of all social lessons: Only when someone tells me what to do and makes me do it, only then can I have this most modest, most humble, most unsatisfyingly small chance to succeed. See how unworthy I am. See how incapable I am of making it on my own without some powerful figure standing over me every step of the way. If, in spite of all that help, I fail, then that just proves how dull and inadequate and incompetent I am. If I succeed, then I owe it all to luck or to the benign authority who stood over me and made me succeed (strict-but-fair teacher, kind boss, politician-with-a-heart-of-gold). The authorities know how weak and helpless I am. How kind of them to help me. I am helpless. There is nothing I can do to help myself.

I tried other directions.

Many of the least productive children enjoyed science. Science in this instance meant not formal lessons but broad amorphous explorations in subject matter that could be loosely identified as science. They did not keep records nor did they pursue any given activity except rather superficially. But they enjoyed planting and taking care of their plants. They were curious about the differences in plants. They could let themselves ask questions about seeds and molds and seedlings which they would never have tried in a formal lesson. Pursuing their interest, I brought in whatever filmstrips or films were available and seemed relevant to their science pursuits. Because there were few formal demands made of the children in these activities, they could relax and enjoy them. They were not, after all, "learning" in school terms, with work to be turned in and knowledge to be held accountable for and marks to be earned.

The lessons spread farther and farther afield. Plants led to animals. Animals led to dinosaurs and the history of the earth, and to volcanoes and rocks and deserts. Animals led to people. All along the way there were stories to be read, books to be explored, fascinating discussions to be held. We sat for hours one day reading the dry text of the encyclopedia about bees, and discussing what we read. Do bees feel respect for their Queen? Do they ever do something besides what they're supposed to? What if—? What if—?

They liked to write stories. If they had trouble writing them, I tried to find time to let them dictate the stories to me. I rarely asked them to rewrite a story. We printed copies for everyone, little magazines that included something from almost everyone in the class. They did their own corrections on their own papers. If I could not go over the story with each one, I would write misspelled words on tiny slips of paper and clip them to the sheet. They would then have to hunt and erase and insert. It was important to them that the corrections be made invisibly. Red pencils made them tense.

We played all kinds of games with sentences, thinking games, riddling out the secrets of syntax, discovering nonsense and sense, discovering that often there was no right answer but many many options instead. That half the children would not bother to do the follow-up practice concerned me, but I had come to expect that. For now I was willing to settle for their participating in the open oral activity.

Lessons with formal structure and demands were far less successful. Putting things down on paper continued to threaten them. Following up something in math, I wrote some exercises for all to do. This gave me the opportunity to go around the room helping children individually. But the structure fails where it most should succeed. The fast workers brought their work to be checked, the slower ones handed in their papers at lunchtime, the bottom—failure avoiders, not necessarily the incapable ones—never got far into the task at all. I was lucky if they managed simply to copy all the numbers down. So it was a failure again. (Maybe a teacher-aide could have helped, checking the output of the voracious ones—because, after all, they need to be checked and credited or to have some small difficulty cleared up—while I concentrated on helping the helpless.)

Penmanship most of them seemed to enjoy. I showed them a modified italic handwriting. There were always two or three little girls (and boys!) enamored of the curlicues of the Palmer method, or whatever the loopy hand is we are supposed to teach. But most children, especially the boys, enjoyed the relatively easy mastery of italic, as well as its elegance and legibility.

In math and to some extent in language arts I tried to get hold of or make materials that did not involve writing. Writers on education for kids from the economic ghettos talk about a "difference in learning styles," the need to work concretely. But from what did the "style" emerge?

Maybe another explanation for the success of manipulative materials (blocks, beans, cards, rods, whatever) is that handling materials is fluid and transient. There is nothing in writing, no evidence of errors permanently recorded. I was checking a paper of Freddy's one day, some silly math drill. He spotted an error before I did and said, "Oh, that should be twenty-four." So I wrote the number twenty-four down and checked it as correct. He could not understand this. If it was wrong as written, what difference did it make that he really knew the answer and had spotted the mistake? I tried to show him the difference between his kind of error and a "real" one, but he did not think I made sense. What's down is down and doomed.

But with the manipulative materials, the same rules do not apply. "Cheating" for once is guilt-free. Cheating as usual meant comparing your own with someone else's work. In school as in the playground, cheating, if caught, is bad. But fumbling around with materials, making changes and adjustments, is somehow different. Besides you can see the others fumbling, making and correcting errors, all at the same time. Of course the need to check with someone else interferes with one's own learning. But more risks are taken, more learning goes on than under the regular class conditions of write-it-down and hand-it-in. And I could devise, on the spot, individual variations so that the kids would be more on their own.*

* Gattegno's *Words in Color,* which I learned about much later, also seems to bear in it the seeds of independence. Teachers tend to dismiss the program as just another "phonic approach." But where many linguistic and pro-

Yet even when we seemed to be functioning most smoothly, the problem of meeting all the children's needs seemed, and still seems, insurmountable. Nobody seems to know what a viable class size is. Certainly for some children the group could be huge—if they were all motivated to achieve success and if the materials were rich and abundant enough. But for the avoiders of failure a small class seems to make more sense. They need an informal class with more than one adult. They need not so much an inundation of materials—they might find such wealth threatening if presented all at once—as an inundation of attention.

Many special programs devised to help so-called ghetto children have not come up to expectations. It may well be because the programs have not coped with and have refused to recognize, in many instances, the problems arising from attitude. The materials change, the activities seem to change: but the child does not.

Even the practice of having a failing child repeat a grade is meant to be a help to him. But in no school where I have worked has the heldover child been treated as anything but someone who needs more time, another chance to catch up. For a very few children the time is a valuable gift; for children who have had special problems to overcome—a second language, or a series of inexperienced and inadequate teachers. Many of the avoiders of failure are, predictably and sooner or later, holdovers. But for them the extra year is a

---

grammed materials seem to make children dependent on the particular environment, *Words in Color* by its very careful structure and its methodology seems to give the children a feeling of independence and confidence, which they so desperately need. Watch children attack a strange word under usual conditions and after two or three errors turn their eyes upward toward the ceiling and fire off a series of wild guesses. Then watch them with Gattegno's color charts, going back and forth, piecing together the clues, shushing anyone who tries to tell them, until they come up trimphantly with the right sound for the word. Or watch them make the unselfconscious discovery that if you cover up the *s* in *sand* the rest of it is just like *and*! What is important is that it is their very own discovery, their very own action in searching and sounding that has produced the desired result.

punishing experience. For the classroom they find themselves in is much like the one they left. Only this time their classmates, who are learning, are a year younger then they. All that the extra year gives them, most of them, is a reinforced feeling of failure and inadequacy.

The schools in New York City give the child three such opportunities to catch up, once at each level, apparently thereby fulfilling whatever obligation they feel toward the nonlearners. If the kids fail again—and they will—it's their own fault. They had their chance and obviously *they* muffed it.

What about a heterogeneous mix of students? The rationale is that it is more stimulating and less psychologically crushing for the children to be in unlabeled classes. Actually the mix is meant for teachers. If you do not have a class identifiably slow, you will not treat the class with low expectations and resignation. But teachers conditioned to the teacher-dominated classroom find the heterogenous group extremely difficult to work with. Often what these teachers see as a more stimulating mix is an illusion. The number of nonreaders touted as "having artistic talent" is appalling.

I worked as a cluster teacher one year. This meant that in addition to covering various classes while the "real" teacher was having her free preparatory period, I would also assist her by working with some of her children in or out of the room. One day, sitting in on a math lesson, waiting to help, I watched the regular teacher interact with the five or six "bright" children, those willing to raise their hands, supply answers, keep the lesson moving. She kept nodding and beaming at me: *See, the class is learning, isn't it a bright class, lively, interested?* Meanwhile most of the children were plodding along, falling farther and farther behind or dropping out of the lesson completely. Some girls were fooling around and I went over to sit with them to help them. They were quite willing to accept my help, but the teacher brusquely announced that they did not deserve special treatment. After all, they hadn't been paying attention all along.

Avoidance of Failure

So the stimulating mix aspect of heterogeneity can be the opposite. The bright and confident children may even be perceived as threatening. They are always measurably *there,* reminders of what I don't know and cannot do. The "bright" children are like raisins in a loaf of unleavened bread. They introduce flavor and are highly visible. They can encourage the teacher in whatever game of self-deception is useful at any given time, from (a) the illusion that the class is learning on the evidence of the participating handful to (z) the illusion that the children who are not learning are problems or ineducable because after all the class is being successfully taught on the evidence of (a).

Maybe we could sort out classes by motivation. Then the avoiders of failure would still be a heterogeneous mix. They are heterogeneous. Their level of permissible performance seems always to be receding from their reach, like Tantalus and the waters. Always they manage to perform short of success at a level of comfortable noncombativeness. At least that is one explanation of how the ghetto school statistics seem always to end up two or three years below whatever the grade norms are, at any level.* Perhaps better, look more closely at the middle-class kids who, not being blessed with a disadvantaged environment, manage instead to "underachieve."

The failure avoiders are not stimulated by the standard school externals. The rewards of competition and praise, and of promotion into a more difficult group, are not really rewards but are clearly and correctly seen as threats. In the same way that my son in fifth grade refused to admit to reading books, accepting thereby his teacher's disapproval, because admission brought with it the need to write book reports or make book jackets or posters or shoebox dioramas, so the children see that success has its penalties in increased expectations and heavier duties. And they know, deep inside, that they can't perform. It was, remember, only luck or a benign

* The fact that the minimum possible score rises with the advancing tests is another.

authority that gave them success. What will they do on their own? Success is full of danger.

I compare the failure avoiders with, say, Shelley. Shelley is insatiable when it comes to neatly defined tasks that involve detailed record-keeping and high output. She has a need to be visibly productive. She and Seth and John and Maria are self-imposing hard taskmasters. They could flourish in the structured clerical atmosphere typical of middle-class schools. Informal learning, for Shelley as for Seth, is indecent and illegitimate, a waste of time. Is it really work if it is fun? Is that what we are here for?

But the avoiders need that very kind of work. They need learning situations that least of all resemble what they know about school: learn, record, report, be marked and labeled and sorted into identifiable groups. Instead they must have more and more materials to explore, introduced gradually over the course of the year so they have time to get to know them and be comfortable with them each in turn.

And they need a no-exit supportive innundation of attention. Their only choice must be to-do-and-succeed. They must first and continuously learn success, learn to accept it, to live with it, to believe in it, not be frightened by it. In a way it is success, the feeling of mastery and competence, that permits learning in the sense of permanent possession and transfer of knowledge. Any other kind of learning, by rote and compulsion, will be short-term and fragmented and useless. The children need to be conditioned to success, just as they have been so efficiently conditioned to failure.

They have been infected, as though by a highly drug-resistant strain of virus, with the knowledge that they are bad and they are stupid. Everything in their environment conspires to keep that faith intact, indeed to reinforce it.

Reading *Children Who Hate* (Redl and Wineman), I was struck by how many children in my class showed some of the symptoms. The authors see no hope short of a change in the total environment, at least in regard to the few extremely disoriented children who come

Avoidance of Failure

to them. I have heard eminent educators speak wistfully of the kibbutz experience in Israel. Such talk frightens me. It is an admission of failure, for one thing. For another, it seems contemptuous of people. Will we take the parents with the children to the new American kibbutz? Or do we assume that these parents will be glad to be rid of them? And will we take with us to the great American kibbutz our present goals and curriculum?

Or some people say their parents must be reeducated. So the schools give workshops, telling parents how to provide a quiet place for homework and how to help the child with reading and math. But who will educate OUR parents? Who will go back into the dark swamps of our own lives, to muck about there and tease apart the twisted roots from which we grew? Where is the school that will teach us, the teachers, to be whole and human?

If our children are suspicious, with no self-control or inner resources, if their relationships with adults have been largely punitive and rejecting, if they are self-centered and impulsive—we can go down the whole mournful list of Redl's twenty-eight symptoms—then what?

If this is what their environment has done to them, is it not time to consider that the schools, and those of us in them, have been a part of that environment? Redl says their egos need restructuring. They need to be healed. But are we, in practice, healers, or fit to be?

Look at Ann, in her sick pursuit of humiliation and failure. She was growing up this way without even the burden of being black to compound her troubles. Now that was all she knew. That was how she related. That was how she was comfortable. It was all too easy, with her help, to humiliate her. But it made no sense to be sucked into her twisted games. How best to get her to learn more without indulging her sick needs? How to help her bear the unbearable anxiety she felt when she could not relate in her accustomed ways?

Or Carl, or George. If I related to the one punitively or to the other oversolicitously, I was strenghthening their weakness and feeding their rationalizations of why they could not learn: Carl because he was picked on and persecuted and hated, George because I confirmed again that he was so inadequate that he needed special treatment and excuses.

I could not restructure their personalities. I'm no therapist. Neither are the guidance counselors. All I could do was try to get education to take place in as spiritually healthy an environment as I could create, without pressure, without value judgments. And I had to insist on their participation, to force them to succeed over and over. Such a conditioning process might leave its mark by year's end. Maybe it would be enough of a mark in their conscious or unconscious so that it would cause a healthy conflict with their accumulated past evidence of failure and wickedness and inadequacy. Maybe the next year it would be a little easier for them to go on.

Anyway, the role of the guidance counselors in the schools should not be in the area of ineffective pseudotherapy and file-keeping. More likely it should be in the area of classroom management. If the classroom really is, as they keep telling us, a punitive atmosphere, then they damn well should be concentrating on making it something else.

The freer classroom, at least, is a beginning. There is, for all its multiple activities going on at once, no place for the teacher or the child to hide. Their mutual, self-serving games of deception cannot be sustained year after year in such a classroom, as they are now.

The freedom which seemed at first to be a threat to adult and child alike became for me that year a necessity without which the delicate and complex work of learning could not very well take place. The failures I had that year were not the failures of the idea. They were due in part to my inability to understand soon enough problems I was encountering for the first time out in the open, problems that had so long been hidden from me. Or else they were the result of my failures of will, which had made for so much inconsistency and timidity.

JULIO

I asked Julio what he had learned this year. He stood quiet for a moment, eyes searching the ceiling, the far walls. Then he said, "Last year I used to say—I can't do it. Now I say—Well, I will try."

SUPERVISORY MEMORANDUM

Black and Puerto Rican Culture and Heritage

. . . .

3. At least once a day each teacher will make specific reference to a person, achievement, creative endeavor, product, scientific accomplishment, historical event, current event, etc. Such a reference must be closely related to the work being taught in a curriculum area noted in his or her plan book.

    The reference will be noted in the teacher's plan book. Every curriculum area offers limitless possibilities for such references and the curriculum area should be varied daily to provide our children with the broadest possible spectrum of ethnic pride and accomplishment.

    Each of the major ethnic groups represented by our pupil population should receive proportionate representation and treatment.

    Supervisors are directed to assist teachers in every way possible in this endeavor to assure a meaningful, creative, vitalized approach and successful program.

. . . .

Once again, our ethnic groups should be adequately and proportionally represented.

Yours truly,

. . . .

Principal

THE MODEL BULLETIN BOARD

"Afro-Americans Who Made Their Mark On the 60's"
Thurgood Marshall, Supreme Court Justice
Patricia Harris, Ambassador
Jane Bolin, Judge
Frederic E. Davison, General
Edward E. Brooke, Senator
Arthur Ashe, Tennis Champion
Gordon Parks, Author, Photographer
Robert C. Weaver, Cabinet Member

8

ONE WORLD

Seth looked up Israel in the encyclopedia. "Look at all them Jews," he said with awe, showing me a photograph of a modern street scene. In his world, he and his family were a minority of one. Then he looked up *Seth* which referred him to Adam and Eve. Did they really live nine hundred years? Adam and Eve meant nothing to him, although some of the children who belonged to fundamentalist sects were familiar with the story. He went to the library to take out books about the Jews and about their holidays. He read and read them. He was learning something fascinating about himself.

Some things are so embedded in our own life context that we find it inconceivable that they (Adam and Eve, the meaning of an inch) are completely meaningless to a child.

But it is surprising and even shocking to discover what the children have learned about their world. As long ago as 1957, on the Lower East Side, a Spanish child recounted a nightmare in which the bad guys were the Red Chinese. Most children have relatives or know of someone in the army, but they are not sure who the enemy is. In spite of television, they have only the most confused ideas about the war in Vietnam. They make guesses: the Japanese are the enemy. Maybe the Chinese. The Germans, the Italians, the Russians. Seth, having discovered his past, cannot conceive of anyone but Germans being the enemy.

They do not watch television news, but they love monster movies and gothic soap operas and adventure series. Subjected as they are to the incoherent, unchronological jumble of films on television, they are exposed to a hodgepodge of conflicting indoctrinations. The Russians are friends, enemies. The Chinese are good-bad; so are the Japanese. The Germans are monsters and buffoons and allies. But under all the superficial variations run some clear threads. By the time they reach high school they will have had a lifetime of indoctrination in the right FEELINGS. They will possess the right set against the undefined enemy, an empty set ready to be filled with whatever the current political needs decree. They will be equipped, at an unconscious, unverbalized level, with all the appropriate rigidities, mystiques, and values. The simplistic platitudes that pass for history in the elementary schools will reinforce what they have learned from television. The world will be a Manichaean universe: good and evil, Uncle vs. Thrush, Kaos vs. Control, I Spy vs. the Commies. They will have acquired an unshakeable faith in our side as the good guys and in our invincibility.

The school books conspire to keep them in ignorance. Time and again they come up with the romantic stereotypes. One year in Queens we analyzed the plots in a fifth-grade reader. Many of the stories involved a boy or girl who wanted something, who was confronted with an adult-stumping problem, who resolved it and was rewarded. Western boys wanted horses; Mexican boys wanted shoes; Dutch boys wanted to win ice-skating races, and predictably, the little African boy only wanted a friend, a white friend.

In social studies, the children learn about the world more directly: Dutch kids in wooden shoes, Arabs in flowing robes on camels, tribal Africa with thatched huts and never a city or car in sight. On occasion we used the Urban Kit, an astonishing collection of audio-visual aids designed to inform the children about, among other things, Minorities Who Made America Great. I am thrilled to discover, in among the pasta and the Joe DiMaggios (the strips are all-inclusive), that it was really an Italian who wrote the Declaration of Independence, only his draft got burned, I think. The history of the Negroes is very thorough; but among the pictures depicting the horrors of slavery is one identified as a slave malingering in order to sabotage his hated condition. He is lying on the floor in rags. A beautifully dressed white doctor is kneeling solicitously at his side. Another picture shows the freed slave sitting by his fireside strumming a guitar or banjo, while the record accompanying the material speaks of his efforts to improve his lot. (I have, seared in my soul, Old Abe lying before the fire place, trying to read. No banjo strumming for Lincoln.) The kit is well-intentioned and, being new, may improve in time.

We were going to look at the Irish strip one day in my experimental class but it had disappeared. So we talked instead about what the children knew about the Irish. They told me about leprechauns and costumes and songs. Several mentioned "talking funny," rolled r's as an example. Did they know any real Irishmen? Three said that they did but they kept insisting that they talked differently from other people. They did not mention our chief custodian, who treasures a brogue. They cited a teacher from Brooklyn who speaks graciously and impressively with broad A's. They admired her speech and sometimes imitated it. They mentioned a little boy lately come from Boston to our neighborhood. As a matter of fact he is not Irish but Jewish. They were very interested in that fact. The Jews they know do not fit in with their stereotypes of Jewishness. They have firm ideas on the subject. All teachers are Jewish. Children are not.

As is usual the children in the class had little opportunity in their neighborhood to check stereotypes against reality. What little real knowledge they possessed of other people rarely is used to break down the stereotypes.

One of the books I read to the children was a biography of Amos Fortune. It came highly recommended as a book that would enlighten the children about Black History. Except for the first few chapters, it was most unsatisfactory. It made such a virtue out of the dreadful necessities of that poor man's life. It was so full of Victorian piety about a life of hard work for small rewards of the uncle Tom sort. I found it unbearable and irrelevant. Toward the end I did more synopsis than reading.

But in the beginning, we discussed the chapters on the slave trade at some length. One day we were discussing the pits where the shackled slaves were kept for weeks waiting for the ship to pick them up. We were talking about the misery, the heat, no water, no movement, no bathroom. Freddy began to giggle like any proper middle-class child and John muttered, "You only think it's funny cause you ain't colored."

I suggested that the children draw illustrations for the story so far. Estabania and the other girls, with Diana's invaluable help, drew tribal dancers: hula girls and Indian braves. The boys drew raiders crouched behind trees. (Just as accurately, another class illustrating the story of Harriet Tubman drew beautiful blondes in frilly gowns looking at the night sky, where one huge star was invariably labelled "North Star.")

Remembering John's sad comment, we discussed other people's travail: the Indians destroyed by the conquerors of Puerto Rico, the Jews in the concentration camps. The children were shocked. "Didn't any of them fight back?" asked Seth.

Didn't they fight back? Seth's question was the standard reaction of identification and shame and anger. Why did they let it happen to them? Black children ask the question about the slaves, Puerto Ricans about their Indians. They want to be told that some people did fight. They want to know that slavery and death did not come because of docility, cowardice, inferiority. Slavery and genocide mean to them not so much the viciousness of the conquerors as it does the weakness and inferiority of the victims. Adults should not be weak, they seem to say. They shouldn't let these things happen to them. But they know that adults are weak and powerless. When they had examples of adults who do fight back, like Malcolm X or the Panthers, they pretended that they had not heard of them. Or one or two children would quote their parents' criticisms of them as lawless troublemakers. Like the Afro haircut, the new black consciousness was very slow in seeping in.

Black children who can will instead boast of remote Indian ancestry, and so will the adults. For them the noble savage survives, an intact myth they can take pride in.

Sometimes when I begin reading a story like Amos Fortune or Ann Petry's excellent life of Harriet Tubman, I find that the children grow tense. They do not know what my purpose is in reading it. They expect only terrible reminders of a past they do not know but are ashamed of. They turn away their heads, in the beautifully symbolic gesture of the ghetto: if I am not looking at you, then I cannot hear you.

One little girl resisted the story of Harriet Tubman for a long time. "You gonna read that book again?" We were midway through the book before she finally came to terms with it. After the day's reading, she came up shyly and put a piece of candy in my hand. After that she did not turn her head away, and often after the reading would tell stories about her own private life, about attending the church where her grandfather was a minister and where, at the end of service, she would pass the collection basket. Her truce was a long time in coming. For most children the tension dissipated quickly. The most restless of nonreaders would sit motionless in engrossed silence, shushing others dictatorially if they had the misfortune to sneeze.

After we had read of all the remarkable accomplishments of Harriet Tubman, I described her one day as a genius. They loved her story and admired her, but genius, they insisted, she was not. She couldn't read or write. They have learned in school that if you can't read you must be stupid. Intelligence = Reading. A prerequisite for being a genius, maybe the only one, is education.

Late in the year we had our annual vestigial shelter drill.

Afterwards we talked about it. ("Why were they all looking at us when we went in the auditorium?" "We were the last ones in and we were rather noisy.")

What was the drill for? I said it was a leftover scheme to protect us from the consequences of nuclear attack and that it was therefore ridiculous. In spite of all the science fiction films, or maybe because of them, the children have added nuclear weapons to the armory of standard weapons of war. They have not placed them anywhere in the scale of time and destructiveness. We attribute the impatience and unrest and escapism of the current generation of young people at least in part to their having grown up with the threat of the bomb. How much more terrifying it is to consider that the next generation is growing up *without* the threat. The Bomb rests comfortably in the closets of their minds among the bows and arrows and tommy guns and hand grenades.

I justified to them, and rationalized to myself, participation in a futile drill because it serves us as practice for other more manageable emergencies. I told them of an incident in my son's high school when the building had to be emptied in haste because of a reported gas leak. Seth, dreadfully literal as always, replied that if we had a gas leak a shelter drill that kept us inside the building would not help us at all.

Freddy, still contemplating the power of the bomb, said we should use it in Vietnam. Even if it meant losing a lot of lives? Sure, even American lives. Say you killed fifty thousand Americans when you dropped the bomb, but the war would be over. It is strange that when people think about and condemn peace-at-any-price, they never seem to include Freddy's solution.

One sunny afternoon, emerging from school, I found a crowd of children surrounding a wino asleep on the sidewalk. He is known as the Professor, an old man with red cheeks and white curly beard. The children made a ring around him, mocking him as he slept. Some boys danced up to him and spit on him. Julio, laughing and excited, joined in. I chased the kids away but I became a part of their game as they darted in behind me to resume their sport. At last a police car pulled up. The cops tried to rouse the old man but could not. One of the policemen picked up the half-empty bottle and emptied it delicately, at arm's length, into the gutter. Then they loaded him into their car and drove off. The children dispersed but Julio lingered. He was still bubbling over with excitement, full of the feeling of daring the wretched game had given him. At last as he talked and I asked questions, he sensed my disapproval. He pouted in what he conceived to be the appropriate expression of contrition and promised: "I won't do it no more. Next time I help him. I chase the kids away. I beat 'em up." He pounded his fist in the air, demolishing cruel enemies by the score. He was off into a fantasy world as insensitive as the real one.

During Thanksgiving week this year, my Third-grade children were bored with doing "What am I thankful for?" "We did that with the sub," they announced. So we made up a list of what they are not thankful for. People who throw beans, death, war, the dying of people who ain't on our side, people going in the garbage to look for food, junkies and addicts and winos and drunks, car accidents, dynamite and things that hurt you, going to the hospital.

From an esthetic point of view, their real world is as appalling as the bloodless antiworld of their school books.

THE GIRLS

Shelley often asked me for an assignment. "What else can I do?" Sometimes it seems as though the children who were best adjusted to school are the ones most at a loss when given choices and small freedom. The good little girls like Shelley devise school-oriented tasks for themselves. They find the dullest of workbooks and work away at them, day in and day out, or the programmed texts that lock them into a fixed and predictable procedure and can be checked for correctness each step of the way. They devise strange homework for themselves, copying whole stories out of books for the sheer pleasure of covering dozens of pages in a notebook. But they seem to lack curiosity. They never ask questions. They are content in class discussions to sit in watchful attentive silence. Only their pleasure at being chosen monitor or being allowed to draw gives a clue to repressed feelings. For a long time they wait for the teacher to select them for special rewards, not bold enough to ask permission for themselves but also secure in the knowledge that all teachers, sooner or later, reward the good children in this fashion.

In late winter I discovered that they had suddenly broken loose from their quiet moorings. For weeks on end they were untidy, chattering, unproductive. It did not really happen suddenly. It was only I, upholder of the faith in structure and patterns, who failed to notice them coming apart at the seams. Where most of the boys were in September they arrived at, giggling and rather impressed by their daring, in March. Workbooks were dull. Homework was nonsense, to be done only on rainy days. Nothing was very interesting. They gave their opinions in class discussions, harsh and contemptuous evaluations gently and hesitantly voiced. They formed and reformed alliances based on arts and crafts, dolls, clothes, attitudes toward boys. And then slowly, quietly, they slipped back to more scholarly ways again, making poetry anthologies, writing stories, reading books for fun, playing math games, the works. The workbooks were never completed. The programmed texts disappeared under all the important current books and papers in their neat desks.

Now, at year's end, their test scores have leaped not so much reflecting a great increase in reading or math skills as simply an increase in their sense of reality, so that they can add objectivity and judgment to last year's burden of tension, competitiveness and cocksure mechanical thoughtlessness.

More important, they have learned to enjoy learning. They have always enjoyed school. For them it was a place where their virtues were recognized and rewarded. But this year, learning has become the reward.

9

TAKING STOCK

Time in institutional life is distorted. It exists either in highly controlled and measured segments—in school, this period or the next, five minutes till three, three more days to Thanksgiving—or in indefinite glacial ages. The impact of events is not felt immediately. Occasionally the memory of an incident and its meaning surfaces like a boulder brought up out of the rivers of ice. Then the grinding small movements bury it again.

The sense of movement and progress is distorted too. In the actions of twenty or thirty individuals thrown together arbitrarily for an arbitrary period of time to perform arbitrary tasks, there is much backing and filling, much bumping and ricocheting. And we all carry with us the burden of our first impressions and old misconceptions. We are rarely aware of them or of the need to evaluate and change them. And there is never time to think.

That is why someone coming into the classroom at regular intervals can see changes with greater clarity than the people immersed in the event.

Beyond that there is the constant war of attrition that goes on visibly and invisibly week after week, as the teacher is forced to accommodate to the realities of the system. Accommodate she must. The teacher cannot control the number of children in her class nor the composition of it. She has almost no control over the quantity and quality and availability of supplies and books unless she is prepared to buy them herself. She cannot usually get the support of supervisors for programs that do not conform to the rules. Her schedules must dovetail with the schedules of the rest of the staff. Administrative solutions always have overriding priority over educational ones.

Looking back at the year of the log from the vantage point of two more frustrating years spent in the system, I try to understand the limitations of the freer classroom as I have worked with it in schools in ghetto communities. To try to teach children in any other way has become, for me, unthinkable, in spite of the fact that I have had to bow to superiors and to schedules too often. Would I encourage other teachers to work that way? Yes, yes, yes. Is it an easier way? I don't know. I think, from my own evidence, that what has made it difficult for me has been my reluctance to give up old ways, to commit myself totally to the idea. I inched in, and the inching, I think, caused many of my problems.

It is necessary to look again at what happens in the classrooms of our public schools. On the surface, we are supposedly teaching children, in elementary schools, to read and to do math. Superimposed on these two basic skills are a load of subject matter—science, art, social studies, and so on—and some all-purpose civic and psychological goals: mental health, good citizenship, etc.

Well, the schools have had an appalling rate of failure in teaching children to read and multiply. Failing in these basic skills, the schools have failed also, for large numbers of children, to teach the other subjects too. And as to the personal goals, it is puzzling to discover what the schools have really taught, beyond the slogans compartmentalized, like commercials, about brotherhood and democracy and free speech.

In a bad mood one day, I cataloged the attitudes that the authoritarian school inculcates in children.

Children learn in school that nonconformists are emotionally disturbed children who must be referred to the guidance counselors (or later on, suspended). Children learn very early to equate individualism, eccentricity, aggressive behaviour in one's own defense with other nonconforming behavior that may be symptomatic of a truly crippling maladaptation. Nonconformists are crazy. Rebels are sick. What a useful equation that is!

Children learn that people fit in boxes and that you behave toward them, and they toward you, in appropriate, box-determined ways. You do not treat winos or junkies or people on welfare or lunchroom aides or children the same way you treat teachers and principals.

Children learn that feelings must be distrusted and that we must learn to deal in words. If you learn the right words, then it does not matter what you really mean or what you do. Children learn that civility is more important than justice. The right words politely spoken take priority over the truth spoken in anger.

Children learn that authority always wins.

Children learn exceptions to the rules. Equality, but not for me. Civil rights and constitutional rights, but not for me. Equal opportunity. Anybody can succeed—if they work hard enough. So if I don't succeed either I didn't work hard enough or I wasn't good enough.

Children learn that cooperation, by school definition and practice, always means the postponement of one's own individual needs and desires. Cooperation means the repression of one's healthy self-assertion.

Children learn that success in school is the gift of authority and that authority gets the credit for it, while failure is purely and completely earned by themselves. Failure means stupidity, incompetence, inferiority. Another useful equation.

Children learn that you must compete or die. Many choose death. But the others are learning that only the best—the top score—will be rewarded. All men, therefore, are your enemies. They are all fighting with you for top place. The world is divided into Top Place and No Place.

Children learn to defer to experts and to distrust themselves. What they know and want to know are of no value. The teacher defines the tasks and decides what the correct answers are, and you are given the choice of accepting her judgments (no matter that she got them from someone over her) or failing.

The children learn that work is not pleasurable or useful. As soon as teachers discover any work that is pleasurable and rewarding, they promptly label it play and both limit its occurrence and drown it in guilt.

Children learn the slogans and rituals of a two-dimensional world: Right and Wrong.

Children learn in school that life is a series of dull and boring tasks from which no one can escape except by failing or withdrawing, and even then they must serve out the minimum years of their prison term. Success is only accompanied by harder tasks of the same kind and more years added on to the sentence.

We teach children to know failure and impotence.

I will grant that it was a bad day. But given the failure of the schools to accomplish their goals and giving the schools more credit than some would allow for the failures of our citizens to cope with the problems of our times, I think that we must go back and question the visions themselves when we talk of redesigning our schools. For most of the reforms that have been put forward in recent years have been like the changes in automobiles, something new each year, superficial elements of style that do not come to grips with the basic problems and needs of a population that must be moved.

The difficulties I encountered and continue to encounter in trying to work in a free classroom are real difficulties indeed. But the problems have always existed. The silent busy classroom has always served to mask the problems, to hide the failures. In spite of all the criticism of the schools for their failures and the efforts to rectify them, the problems seem to be exacerbated, because the solutions are stop-gap and frivolous, or because the professionals are afraid, or because we do not really clearly see what the problems are, or lack the will or the energy to tackle them We are forever, we educators, curing typhoid by administering aspirin to diminish the fever, and the results are predictable.

One of the lesser problems I encountered was and still is one of adequate materials and books. A rich supply available to the teacher and her children would simplify some of the problems of the first, unfamiliar weeks. With the freedom to choose we must also provide options appealing to the children. Happily, more and more useful and imaginative supplies are becoming available from a variety of sources here and abroad. Teachers must become adept at finding them buried as they are by the flood of shiny gimmicky junk in the approved lists and catalogs, and must practice the art of getting supervisors to order them, from the limited funds available.

A more difficult problem is administrative inflexibility. Principals do not have the authority, at least in New York City, to manipulate class sizes, to hire and use staff except according to severely defined limitations—even if the principals had the vision and will to work outside these limitations.

Custom is a chain to bind us. The problems of failure in the ghettos are acknowledged. But it is much cheaper to pour millions into special programs that bustle in the corridors of the existing schools, pulling teachers out of the classrooms to run them. The problems of failure, as I discovered in my room, were neither so difficult nor so simple to solve. As Gattegno says, to teach children who have learned how to speak the far easier task of learning to read is not difficult. What presents the seemingly insurmountable difficulty is to teach children who have learned how to fail the far more vital lesson of how to succeed, after which the rest is easy. The free classroom is only the first step for those children who have already mastered failure.

I cannot, I think, put the case too strongly for the needs of the children who have failed. It is not enough to say they need remedial lessons and one-to-one relationships and relevant readers. It is wrong to blame the environment from which they came, or motivation, or poverty, if only because the school cannot now do anything about the world outside and such ready excuses distract us from the task within. The free classroom promises that the burden of failure will not be increased. But within it, there are special demands that must be met, if the children are not to fail again. We must mix with freedom the support and insistent attention that the children who are failing need. This means that for them there is no easy solution to be found in programmed instruction, skills stations, open classrooms, Skinnerian rewards (with their frightening outgrowth, contracted instruction in which greed is the motivation and *things* are the payoff). The programs will not work or will work with only limited and short-range success unless they are accompanied by the constant attention and protection that the children need and that they can only get in very small classes with enough adults to serve them.

Dr. George Wald once said that the test for all foreign and domestic policy should be, simply: "Is this good for the children?" How much more so should the test be applied to the schools?

The free classroom *is* good for the children. It does not prevent them from being children. It does not stop them from learning in their own way, the only efficient way for each individual. It teaches them *how* to learn, and not *what* to learn. It expands their curriculum to include the most important subject of all: themselves, as people learning to master their environment and thereby their lives. It teaches children the lessons of freedom in the only way these lessons can be taught: through the exercise of it, with all the responsibility and accountability, all the room for mistakes and successes, all the testing of limits and of needs, growing out of the world of the child. It allows the adults in that world to become at last the protectors instead of the oppressors of childhood.

THE LAST DAY

The children revert
to childhood.
Our fantasied trolls
who tormented us
all year—vanished;
cast out, the devils
who clamored at our souls
taunting us with obscene pleas
to be let in.

Freed from our prison
for a day,
they are transformed
by laughter.

The tough man-child
came and planted a soft kiss
on my Judas cheek—
I who have so often betrayed him.

II

> *"The only thing that can become fate for a man is belief in fate. . . . And to be freed from belief that there is no freedom is indeed to be free."*
>
> I and Thou
> *Martin Buber*

10

THE TEACHER—AGAIN

I had returned to the log, "to the notes written in anger and contempt and concern, to try to discover what I, *a teacher*, am." But the log is not enough.

I have used the term *authoritarian* to describe the kind of education I oppose. The structure of the school system is authoritarian and so is its intent. But most teachers would insist, with accuracy, that they are authoritarian neither by intent nor disposition. They are right, of course, or else we would not have so many problems with disruptive and rebellious children. If the majority of teachers were authoritarian we would not need policemen in the halls of our schools.

Why is it, then, that the only subject we continue to teach successfully is failure? More importantly, what happens to us when we fail? For our children's failure is in a larger sense our own. If they cannot tolerate it, if it is destructive for them, then is it no less intolerable and destructive to us?

We are always being handed ready-made excuses for the failure, and we need them—to relieve us of our burden of guilt and helplessness. For example, there is Robert Coles, one of the more humane writers on the subject of education. Coles uses the term *culture shock* to explain why children, in the third and fourth grades, suddenly seem to come to a complete halt. They slow down the already slow rate of progress, they lose interest in school, sooner or later they give up and drop out.

According to Coles, the ghetto and its dreadful promises come into focus for the child. The child knows now, Coles says, that there is no hope for him, no place to go, and he withdraws from the suddenly perceived irrelevance of school.

Be this as it may, something has been happening inside the school itself. In the first grade or the second the child has been trying to learn to read, usually by the sight method, and to some limited extent his working environment has been humane. There are breaks in the routine. Milk snacks and cookies are still provided, as is informal playtime. Most teachers still use art activities as a major part of the curriculum. There is still an emphasis on talk, music, acting, games.

But in third grade the curriculum gets whipped into shape. Children sit at their desks for hours. Notebooks and textbooks become the main focus of their activity. Lessons are formally organized into spelling, penmanship, reading, composition, math. Silence and good behavior are at a premium now as never before. The restless child graduates from being seen as immature (and therefore to some degree tolerated) to being judged as disruptive and as having emotional problems.

Besides this difference in the climate of the classroom, the gaps in learning loom unmanageably large. The child who has not mastered all the intricacies of the numbers through twenty is now expected to learn all kinds of difficult concepts about fractions and multiplication and place values and "exchanging." The odds and ends of sight words that he was expected to have memorized are now clearly insufficient for his needs. What phonic tricks he may have been taught (initial consonants, rhyming words) will not serve him. His nonstandard dialect or native Spanish create problems that his teachers do not recognize. His third-grade books free themselves from the simple redundant syntax of the first two readers and present him with a language full of unfamiliar words and idioms and unfamiliar content and undecipherable syntactic relationships.

The double burden of an increasingly restrictive school environment and an increasingly incomprehensible curriculum prove too much. Failure becomes his daily companion to a degree unnoticed by the adults who teach him.

Instead the teachers point to the environment outside. Teachers and others say the middle-class parents instill in their children a belief in the value of education. Middle-class children can postpone gratification. They work for long-range goals. They know they must study hard so that they can get into college. But do they? Sure, in many families there is the assumption that the child is collegebound. So the children come to put college on their agenda in the same way and with the same resignation that all children put junior high and high school on their agenda. It is simply something they will have to go through.

The real pressure for grades and competition for place, the real work-for-long-range-goals, does not begin until the middle of junior high, when the children recognize that this semester's grades will be counted in one's average for college. Until then, the pressures are more selective and immediate.

The elitism of special classes, the honors and attention and rewards reaped from unusually good work, the sighs and reproaches and deprivations that accompany the failure, that are seen as a betrayal by the parents, these are what goad the children to work. Even failure has its compensations in the middle classes, up to a point. I heard a mother talking on a bus in Queens one day. Her voice was that strange and irritating combination of complaint coated over with self-congratulation. Her high school son had fallen behind in some course or other and had been signed up for special tutorials in the summer. (There's another area for research: the number of middle-class kids who have had private tutoring.) Naturally it was unthinkable that the rest of the family take its Florida vacation as planned. Perhaps he would be lonely. Perhaps he was not to be trusted. But he had further extracted from his sacrificing family the promise of scuba-diving gear AND scuba-diving lessons upon successful completion of his make-up class.

There are, even for the not so bright middle-class kids, the professional and scholastic options: teaching, accountancy, journalism, banking, merchandising, and the scores of small colleges which flood our mailboxes with their thinly veiled promises of low standards, easy work, and a giddy social life. The middle classes do not need open enrollment. They have it already.

I go back again to the child I was. Did I have long-range goals? Did I expect to go to college? Not at all. My family, like most immigrant and ghetto families, valued education for its promise of better jobs than they could get. But neither my parents nor the community at large expected us to go to college. We were poor Italians in a rural community. The school, happily, was indifferent. If you could do college-preparatory work you were assigned to the college-preparatory courses. What you did with your diploma afterwards was no concern of the school. When I got a job in the library after the school day, the WASP ladies used to talk in front of me about how unusual and marvelous it was that *an Italian* should be found shelving books. I read Richard Halliburton and never dreamed in realities.

All I knew, if I thought of the future at all, was that I did not want to be a school teacher. I didn't have the slightest idea what other professions might be open to women, but of this I was sure, teaching was out. I see with a pang of recognition the young black mothers dreaming of going back to school to learn to be nurses. For them, too, teaching is never a viable option.

The psychology of poverty is to a large degree masochistic. You see the people around you working and scrimping and not making it. Or if they do make it they have become so used to the working and scrimping that they don't even know they've made it. Or you build up a backlog of debts and needs and then when you get a small bundle ahead you blow it, as though to give you the spiritual blubber to protect you against the next cold season.

My father, given to grandiose evaluations of life, would announce: *It is Destiny that devours me!* How comforting those ominous words were. It was not his fault that we were in debt and often penniless. It was Fate. Life became for the adults a brutal game of trying to trick or placate a hostile and implacable Destiny.

The fathers tried to con Fate. Mothers tried to placate it. They were the ones who cooked, who washed, who dressed the children. The men fought and lost. The women suffered. We grew up hating our incompetent ineffectual fathers, and hating ourselves for loving them anyway—that was a betrayal of our abused mothers. As for our mothers, we dared not admit that we hated them. We dodged our chores, acted in small rebellious ways to punish them. The rebellions grew smaller as we grew older. The most minute gesture of independence or of rejection was sufficient to crush our already crushed mother and reduce her to tears and long, sad reproachful silences. And after that came the guilt. The guilt filled in all the molecular spaces of our souls, leaving no room at last for anger or hate or love.

Guilt was our destiny and it truly devoured us. When we did well at school we hid our pride in accomplishment deep in the inaccessible reaches of our minds. On the surface we were modest. To a large degree we did not enjoy the credit for our good work. It was both inadequately praised and overly praised. The work came easy, it wasn't therefore of much value. How we treasured our failures and near failures in math or science. We knew we could be brilliant in both if we really tried but we were afraid to try because we knew we could never achieve the success we envisioned. So we treasured our mediocrities as another example of Destiny. If only we were smart in math. If only!

Much as we were aware of our deprivation, we were also contemptuous of success. We took pride in our penury. We made a virtue of necessity, that hideous masochistic trick. We undervalued ourselves but we resented and—dare we say it—hated others. Part of the attraction of tabloid tragedies is the relief that we have been spared, and the grist they provide for the mills of our hostile fantasies. But the other part is the satisfaction of seeing Destiny destroying other, more fortunate people.

Puritanical morality colored all our judgments. We clothed ourselves in righteousness when we had nothing but hand-me-downs to wear. But in another way we did not see ourselves as deprived and *Poor. Poor* is always a pejorative. Other people are poor because they are stupid or incompetent or thriftless. We were p— because of Destiny, and what a grand and satisfying difference that was.

With the arrogance of failure and our secret articles of faith in our superiority-in-adversity, we could clearly see that others made it because of luck or connections, never by their own talents and efforts.

The necessary consequence of that world view was that we could never, by our own efforts, change our world. We drifted into classes and schools and jobs and out of them. Luck was the agent. There was nothing we could do except what we were doing.

Dick Gregory, in *Nigger*, tells of the "kind white lady" bringing a Thanksgiving basket to his door. Because his family has no means of cooking the turkey, he is furious and rejects the whole basket. Gifts can never be disinterested. There is nothing we can do about our condition. There are no options, no neighbor's oven to use. Just our luck again!

Our feelings came from two rivers that perhaps shared the same source: the personal psychology of our parents and the society that rewarded that psychology by granting it limited amnesty. This psychology—of Fate and Luck—was the only safe and nearly tolerable way to relate to a dangerous, unpredictable, unbearable world.

Meeting the black mothers in Peter Cuomo's (Sonny's) luncheonette, where they stop by for a breakfast of coffee and bread on their way to their jobs, I am most impressed with how much they resemble my mother or my maiden aunts. They scrimp and slave and dream hopeless dreams for the children, mixing compassion with laughter and prejudice and superstition. They want love but do not know how to get it except on unacceptable terms. You must love me not because I am human and deserving of love, but because you owe it to me. I have paid for your love by my suffering.

Sustaining them when all people fail them and betray them, as sooner or later they must, is a hard ramrod morality and a faith in God which He has by no means shown Himself worthy of.

In hearing their stories about their lives, I travel back in space and time to my childhood during the Depression. Being black takes all the fun out of masochism.

The profession of teaching, however, seems to be one tailor-made for masochists. It has most of the prerequisites: our father figures are often gratifyingly sadistic. We are asked to perform with all the nobility and dedication of spirit that martyrs love to indulge in. We are guaranteed failure and humiliation and punishment by the nature of our tasks and the rules of the game. We are given the opportunity within the structure to moan to our hearts' content. Most important of all, we are given victims for our sacrifice. The only negatives in the profession, from the masochist's point of view, are the reasonably adequate salary and the more than adequate vacations and the job security. But we manage to find hobgoblins to threaten even these: from the community that will fire us to the proliferation of requirements for licensing and salary raises, which doom us to spend our spare hours in stuffy, dull graduate school classrooms, doing penance for our sins of leisure.

There are a lot of good qualities in masochists. They can work like drones; they are possessed of inhuman amounts of patience; they can endure the unspeakable long after everybody else has fled in despair. But their virtues also contain the seeds of their destruction. They support institutions that should be, if not destroyed, then certainly radically reformed. They tolerate the destruction of the children because they do not know how to fight. In the end, oppressed by their burden of guilt, they rid themselves of it, in self-defense, by participating actively in the destruction of the children.

I know. I've been down that road. Now like an alcoholic on the wagon, I can recognize, with a not very commendable mixture of malice and pity, my fellow drunk anywhere. I talk to young teachers who have come to the schools all full of ideals and hopes and energy. They are beautiful. (All young healthy masochists are beautiful. Peace Corps people are beautiful. Young people in communes are beautiful.) I listen to the words begin to turn sour on their lips and I want to shake them and say, "Wait, wait, you don't have to travel that road. You can choose to be free."

I don't mean to make a parlor game of it. It is much too important for that. I see the young teachers betraying their own best feelings about children and the classroom, helpless victims not only of the system but of themselves. I hear them reject the free classroom because they "can't stand the noise," or accept all the sociological explanations in the same spirit that Noah took the news about the flood: *Sauve qui peut* and I can't save everybody. I watch them fall into the standards and jargon and rituals of the approved classroom or caught in the trap of rage at the authority above whom they cannot resist and at the children below who persist in resisting them. I see them turn the gift of love into the dreary obligations of duty. And when the children reject them, I watch as love dies, to be replaced by the poison trees of hate and fear.

How do you teach a young adult the difference between guilt and love, between giving and sacrificing, between impotent rage and productive, channeled anger? How can you teach them to forgive themselves and in that act to forgive all others? You don't, no more than you teach children anything at all. You just go on explaining things over and over, in this form and that, in the hopes that some day their need and your lesson will coincide and they will suddenly understand.

One of the less fashionable but still current explanations for the failure of the schools is that there is a culture clash in the schools, between the values and mores of the ghetto and those of the middle classes. But with surprisingly few exceptions, the teachers in our schools were the products of lower-class immigrant culture, just one or two generations back.

America is no longer the land of the immigrants. It is the land of the second and third and fourth generation American. But consider what the immigrants brought with them to this country. The Italians brought their peasant culture of close-knit families, submissive women, dominating men. The Jews brought their closed urban ghetto culture, highly defensive and exclusive. Within their protected places they had learned to nurture a faith in their own superiority to help them withstand the hostile dismembering world outside. The blacks faced with an even harsher world were never permitted the sustaining gift of pride. Their norms have served them poorly, permitting them only survival, and in a sense insuring that they would never be able to rise above that grim level.

For them as for us, the children of the immigrants, the old emotional patterns no longer serve. Our tribal cultures just will not do in megalopolis. Concern for individual-family-tribal-ethnic survival is changed by some wretched alchemy in the open-for-whites society into a narrow and paralyzing conformity.

Emotions that were necessary and comfortable in the Old World are not or should not be necessary in the New. They are, needless to say, not comfortable at all. But we are stuck with them and we don't know it. As we move further and further from the spiritual and material world that produced the emotions, we are oppressed with feelings of anxiety and of loss. The emotions remain but they grow twisted and deformed in an alien environment. A kind but inaccurate simile would be to compare the feelings with a cactus plant set out in a landscape of rich soil and greenery and much rain. In the midst of abundance it must sicken and die.

It is strange that America has served to emasculate its immigrant men and to enhance the guilt-provoking martyrdom of its women.

Now the young are trying to escape the pattern. Their parents and grandparents had to suffer in one way or another to achieve their version of the American dream, paying the price of dull jobs and unfulfilled pleasures, even now paying the most gratifying price of all: the rejection of them by the children for whom they gave everything.

But the young do not have such an easy way to psychic survival, not in a world of affluence. So they have grown up with a huge undischarged debt to their own parents and therefore the world. For many it has become unbearable enough so that they have willingly declared bankruptcy. I leave your values, your world, your debts and obligations, your life without joy. Some of them manage to escape. But too many carry their innocent burden of guilt with them and find in escape only self-destruction. For all their longing to love and be loved, they have never really been allowed to learn how. Maybe that is why there is so much emphasis on the external identifications of style—that's how you can tell that I am one of the lovable ones, that's so I'll be able to recognize you. And they find their enemies: the pigs and the greasers.

The police and the working-class kids (or their elders) still are trying to make it. For them the Old World patterns of emotion still work. But the New World is closing in on them too. The young and their enemies sense in one another threats to their own survival. Their confrontations are really an externalization of the internal conflict between the two sides of the coin. I am still suffering and sacrificing to achieve what you testify is worthless. I don't want to believe you. I cannot afford to believe you, or else what is it all about? And on the other side, the flower children so carefully repress their rage and aggression and so wantonly invite the still accessible rage and aggression of their other, secret selves, whom they have labeled (with a hatred they did not know they were capable of displaying) the pigs and the greasers.

What can we do, we teachers and policemen and flower children and workers, when we are, so many of us, galloping masochists in a society that no longer requires such emotions for its stability and survival? A society, indeed, that needs for its survival people who will refuse to suffer? The tragedy is that destiny truly devours us. It is so hard for us to see what is going on and to understand it and to change ourselves first and then our world. So instead we keep changing the world so that it meets the twisted specifications of our emotions. With safe jobs and our houses bulging with driftwood lamps and matching bedroom sets and stuffed and yielding furniture, how will we suffer now? We manage, for humans are nothing if not inventive. We are pledged to inaction, whether it is the helplessness of "You can't fight City Hall" or the elaborate intellectualizations about the mythical powers of the military-industrial complex or the secret all-powerful manipulative Establishment. Not that these do not exist in some way in objective reality. But it is generations of timidity and helpless self-negating paralysis that have bolstered them. We attribute to them great power and strength when the truth is we have given them the gift of our unused power and unrecognized strength.

How many times have we voted for a candidate we did not like because our real choice had "no chance of winning"? How else explain the "liberals" who will compromise themselves into an about-face rather than fight? Or in the schools again, how else understand why teachers complain most vociferously about the not-so-petty indignities inflicted upon them but, in a showdown, can never find a good enough reason to stand and make a fight? No issue is ever important enough. They are always saving their big guns for a really important issue, they say, while their guns are water pistols, rusting away from disuse.

Thus in our lives we either destroy one another inside the safe walls of home or we create a hostile world outside that is clamoring to destroy us: a punishing world of miserable subways, traffic jams, overcrowding, injustice, air and water pollution, indifferent bureaucracies, unresponsive leaders, war. Our paralysis permits our exploitation. We create and nourish our exploiters.

The enemy grows more numerous and stronger every day, as we narrow our world down to the smallest of insular families. In the vacuum of our impotence, the enemy does indeed multiply, thereby giving the truth to our lies and delusions.

We teach our children not the middle-class values (whatever they are), but our Old World values deformed and misshapen into a reasonable facsimile of what we think middle-class values should be. But more and more our public faces come to be the private faces of our masochistic women. We teach our sons that fighting is bad before we ever let them learn that they can fight to protect themselves, or that they are worthy of defending. We teach them that tears are not manly, but neither is healthy aggressiveness. That is the brute's way. Indeed for many of us the very word aggressiveness has come to have only *bad* connotations. We teach them that they must yield and give of themselves unstintingly as we do, but they know by our example that we keep careful records of indebtedness and obligation that can never be erased. (My father: "I may forgive but I'll never forget.") So they learn that giving is never disinterested, it is always accompanied by the gift of guilt, the product of self-sacrifice and self-denial. It is never the natural outcome of an abundance of joy.

Violence is bad. Anger is bad because it can only lead to violence. Anger must be hidden, denied, suppressed. Self-assertion is bad because it will only lead to confrontations and rejections that will lead to anger, which will of course end in violence. It is no wonder that Buber's philosophy has made so small a mark on the world. It is the glorious rejection of the world of denial and impotence.

We teach our children to be nice and proper and to share and to love-love-love certain selected people. We teach them to hide their feelings in words. We supply them with a vocabulary that becomes more euphemistic and meaningless with each passing year. The attraction of sensitivity-training-institutes-of-joy is surely that of a safe protected place where we can play at having real feelings.

I watched a family at the beach one day. The mother, enjoying surcease from her punishing domestic tasks, was sunbathing. Father was very involved in being father, American style, playing with his children. The children had started to build a sand castle, sloppy and poorly conceived and soul-satisfying. Father came over and helped them create an architectural triumph beyond their puny skills, with much directing and correcting and patient smoothing and shaping. When it was finally done, they sat back on their heels to admire it. The little girl, a three-year-old, toddled over to it and gave the valued monument a whack. The five-year-old boy, basking with his father in the glorious outcome of their shared labor, became enraged, as who would not? He started after the girl but father intervened. Mustn't hit. She's only a little girl. It doesn't matter. *It's only an old pile of sand anyway.*

The boy stormed off, kicking up sand and complaining, but staying well away from sister and castle. By and by he distracted himself. But he was playing alone. Father could not bear the reproach and rejection implied by his isolation

He called him over, and the little girl too, to the now abandoned castle. It's only a pile of sand. We don't like it. Let's bust it. Boom. Let's bust it down.

And the three of them began the terrible game of pseudorage, pseudodestruction, venting the bloodless remnants of their anger and disappointment on a castle now designated as worthless, in a joyless ritual game of pretense.

So that is how it is done. I thought. How sad and terrifying. As the failure-ridden children of the schools have shown us, the hardest lessons to unlearn are the ones we learned unconsciously. The schools, like our parents and our television sets, are the transmitters of culture. But what if a large part of that culture is no longer worth transmitting? What if it has reached that critical point, as our society seems to have done? Do we continue teaching the same paralyzing lessons over and over again? And do we watch as our world is more and more polarized, not between rich and poor or black and white or young and old but between autism and sadism, between violence and withdrawal? Is the civility we desire worth the price of the funeral?

Or do we dare risk life?

Do we, trained to endure the unspeakable, have within us the strength for one more sacrifice, the only one worthwhile? Can we, parents and teachers, set our children free of us?

We judge the turmoil and disruption in our schools and streets as destructive and dangerous. Maybe some of it is. But most of it is not. We condemn it and fear it where we should be nurturing it and performing tribal fertility rites around it. This is the life-force which is exploding from our dry, long-buried, long-dormant seed, the life-force that threatens us with salvation.

Sometimes I think that the only fit motto for our schools is "Abandon Hope, all ye who enter here." It should be "Unless ye become as little children—." Maybe the free classroom will be one of the doors leading into the kingdom of Man.